SYMBOLS OF
CATHOLICISM

Assouline Publishing
601 West 26th Street,
New York, NY 10001
www.assouline.com

© 2000 Assouline Publishing for the present edition
First published in French by Editions Assouline
Les Symboles catholiques © 1996, 1999 Editions Assouline
© RMN photographs p. 17, 19, 29

Distributed in all countries, excluding France,
Belgium, Luxemburg, USA and Canada,
by Thames and Hudson Ltd (Distributors), London

ISBN: 2 84323 188 4

Translated by Ian Monk

Printed in Italy

SYMBOLS OF CATHOLICISM

FOREWORD BY MONSIGNOR DI FALCO
TEXT BY DOM ROBERT LE GALL, ABBOT OF KERGONAN
PHOTOGRAPHS BY LAZIZ HAMANI

ASSOULINE

CONTENTS

FOREWORD

The Catholic religion is an integral part of Western civilization. For centuries, its main festivals (Christmas, Easter and Pentecost) have been landmarks for the family and society, structuring the academic year and our working lives. The culture which we all share is full of expressions which refer to Christ's life and his teachings. Their symbolic significance has diminished because everyday usage has distanced them from their original meaning.

In this book, Dom Robert Le Gall has decided to give them back their true meaning and to explain them with a coherent clarity which makes them accessible to one and all, believers and unbelievers alike. The Catholic faith carries a message of hope and peace, an unshakeable confidence in the love of God and the dignity of mankind. Each day we can see how important these convictions still are in a world scarred by fratricidal wars and by the direct consequences of a deep economic crisis.

In these pages, which are inspired by a constant desire for openness and clarity, all of us will find material that will set us thinking or aid us in our reflections. Those Christians who find themselves once again face to face with the essential elements of their faith will find it strengthened by a clearer understanding of its foundations. Thanks to the visual beauty of the sumptuous photographs which illustrate it, this book will also speak to those who do not share our hopes, for they will see that beauty is the Christian tradition's primary means of expression.

This is a book of reference but also, and above all, a celebration of the mysteries of our faith. It will thus find a home with all those who feel strongly for humanity and who, above and beyond their daily lives, seek spiritual nourishment.

Monsignor Jean-Michel di Falco
CULTURAL ADVISOR AND DIRECTOR OF THE ST LOUIS CENTRE, ROME

INTRODUCTION

SYMBOL AND UNITY

"To the Dearly Beloved Son"

I. CHRISTIANITY AND WESTERN CULTURE
Without at least some knowledge of Christianity, it would be difficult to understand the history of Europe, and even much of world history. Everyone knows who the Pope is, but who really knows about his role as head of the church? Everyone talks about Christmas and Easter, but how many people know the true meaning of these two widely celebrated festivals? European art has been fundamentally Christian for the last two thousand years; in order to understand countless masterpieces, a knowledge of Christian culture is essential. Western painting, sculpture, music, architecture and goldsmithery are all inextricably linked to the "holy story" told in the Bible, which today is still the world's number one best seller.

How do such well known works as Michelangelo's *Moses* in Rome or his *David* in Florence fit into the Old Testament? Without at least a smattering of biblical knowledge, who could decipher a single scene on the stained-glass windows of Chartres Cathedral or of the Sainte-Chapelle in Paris? What is to be made of Johann Sebastian Bach's *St Matthew Passion* without at least a nodding acquaintance with the Gospels?

As we are about to enter the third millennium, the younger generations are feeling the need to rediscover their roots, to breathe a purer air. After the failure of totalitarian regimes, which sought to destroy religion, they are once again experiencing a profound need for spirituality. This desire explains the success of the series of books launched by Editions Assouline. The first volume, *The Symbols of Judaism*, is a beautifully clear presentation of the Jewish religion. The text, by Rabbi Marc-Alain Ouaknin, is both simple and precise. His introduction, which deals with the link between ritual and myth, is close to some of my own analyses of this subject.[1] It is a good thing that the volume on Judaism appeared first, for Christianity is closely connected to it, not only through the Scriptures, but also in its liturgy. Laziz Hamani's superb photographs are more than just a feast for the eyes: they come so close to suggesting a third dimension that one is almost tempted to touch them. They are full of light and vitality, and as such they fulfil their aims to perfection: they do not just act as illustrations but bring the symbols of Catholicism to life.

II. FLESH AND SPIRIT: THE SYMBOL
This is the true nature of any symbol. It is both material and spiritual: concrete reality conveying an unseen truth. The lion, for example, symbol-

8

izes strength, just as the snake symbolizes cunning or the dove peace. The Greek verb *sym-ballo* means "to throw, or put together." The original *symbolon* was a token of recognition or, to be more precise, two tokens which fitted together thus showing the blood-relationship or friendship between the two people who possessed them. The role of the "symbolic" is, then, to bring together and to unify, whereas the "diabolic" separates (*dia-bolos*, from *dia-ballo* "to throw across, to separate or divide"). Symbols are a constant requirement of human nature, which is made up of both a soul and a body. They allow us to pass from the one to the other by means of an image or of a text. Advertising and the media make constant use of symbols. As human beings, we are both spirit and flesh, "incarnated" spirits, and we live on both levels. The flesh, when left to itself, becomes weary; when turned into a symbol alongside the spirit, it is a source of joy and beauty. Conversely, the spirit becomes coldly intellectual when left on its own. By uniting flesh and spirit, symbols make our personal selves whole and allow us to communicate with others. They act as linchpins or hinges and are essential to us. Signs and symbols refer to a reality which transcends them. The difference between them is that signs are more specific, while symbols are richer.

III. SYMBOL AND INCARNATION
Christianity is a religion based on incarnation. Christ, who is at once God and man, is the mediator for our salvation. He took the form of man to allow us to enter into the life of God.[2] This key to Christian symbolism is epitomized by the sacraments, a combination of spoken words and visible signs, which appeal to all five of the senses. Apart from the words which we hear and the gestures which we see, liturgy also makes us smell incense or balm, and taste the bread and the wine which have become the body and blood of Christ (as such, the eucharist is much more than just a symbol, it is the constantly renewed remembrance of Christ's sacrifice). It appeals to the sense of touch through the laying-on of hands and the use of unction, by attending to the sick, caring for the poor and maintaining contact with the dying. God reveals himself and gives himself to us at the most critical moments of our lives, and his religion remains profoundly human.

IV. CHRISTIAN SYMBOL AND UNITY
Symbols unite and bring us together even though Christians do not live in that perfect unity which, before the Passion, Christ asked of God for his disciples.[3] Despite numerous disagreements and ruptures, the Church managed to maintain this unity for a thousand years, for the Great Schism with the East occurred only in 1054. Then, five hundred years later, in the sixteenth century, Luther's Reformation separated the Christians of the West and led to the wars of religion.

The twentieth century, however, has seen an increasing number of ecumenical initiatives and attempts at reconciliation. This is what Pope John Paul II wrote at the beginning of his Encyclical *Ut unum sint* ("May they be one") of May 25, 1995: "The call for Christian unity, made by the Second Vatican Ecumenical Council with such impassioned commitment, is finding an ever greater echo in the hearts of believers, especially as the Year 2000 approaches, a year which Christians will celebrate as a sacred Jubilee, the

commemoration of the Incarnation of the Son of God, who became man in order to save humanity."[4] This book was written by a monk of the Benedictine Order and presents the symbols of the Roman Catholic Church. However, most Christians will find that the symbols it contains will be familiar to them. The sister churches of the East, which are known as "orthodox" (literally "sound in doctrine" in Greek), basically share the same faith and the same sacraments as the Catholic church, expressed in different but complementary ways. While the liturgical reforms promulgated by the Second Vatican Council, and its desire for a return to a noble simplicity in religious services,[5] have regrettably impoverished the signs we use, eastern rites remain richly symbolic.

Roman liturgy is marked by a certain discretion, both in its texts—biblical for the most part—and in its gestures or vestments. But this leads to a powerful expression of the sacred, which is the presence and action of God. In the West, the Anglican and Lutheran liturgies are fairly close to Roman liturgy, while the Reformed Church, more strongly linked to Calvin, is far simpler focussing entirely on the Word of God. In the different chapters of this book, we shall whenever possible draw attention to the importance and the meaning of the symbols in each of the Christian churches.

V. THE POPE:
SYMBOL OF PRINCIPLE AND UNITY
The primacy of the Bishop of Rome and, more generally, the question of ministry may seem like a stumbling block on the road to unification. Christian experience is first and foremost a communion with God, a loving attachment to his word and his will. From Genesis to Revelation[7]

the Bible bears witness to the desire of God the Bridegroom to join himself with his People, the Bride of God; and the love poem *The Song of Songs* expresses all the tenderness which draws them together. Why, then, do human intermediaries interfere in this intimate exchange? There, too, the mystery of the incarnation can enlighten us: Christ, who had come to live among mankind, returned to his Father's side on the day of the Ascension, leaving the church he had set up to carry on his work, so that this Bride might find her full dimension in time and in space. Jesus made Peter and the other eleven apostles the heads of this church so that they might transmit the word and the gifts of God.

The Second Vatican Council clearly showed that the hierarchy of the Catholic church was an integral part of the People of God and at its service.[8] If the Pope, the bishops, priests, and deacons all represent in their various ways the Bridegroom and the Shepherd, they are neither there to replace him nor to serve as substitutes for him, but to guarantee a full and truthful communion with him.

The Pope is an outstanding symbol for Christians, but also for all of our contemporaries, even if, like Christ, he is "destined to be a sign that is opposed" (Lk 2:34). Jesus decided to build his church on the Rock of Peter[9] and it was his responsibility to "strengthen your brothers" (Lk 22:32). As the successor to Peter in the Roman see, John Paul II said in his homily of December 6, 1987, in the presence of Dimitrios I, the Archbishop of Constantinople and Ecumenical Patriarch: "I insistently pray the Holy Spirit to shine his light upon us, enlightening all the Pastors and theologians of our Churches, that we may seek—together, of course—the forms in

which this ministry may accomplish a service of love recognized by all concerned."[10]

The Pope is not the only sign, symbol and principle of church unity. He presides over Charity, alongside his brother bishops, who are themselves assisted by priests and deacons, who are in turn at the service of all their lay brethren as members of the People of God. All are worthy before the mystery of the Church. The poor, in every sense of the word (physical, psychological, economic, social or spiritual), are one of the symbols most cherished by Christians, for they are a reminder that Christ humbled himself and even went to the extent of dying on the cross.

The notion of a symbol is a flexible one. It covers any reality which gives us "food for thought." Catholic symbols include everything which is linked with Catholicism, and not just liturgical objects. Christ, God-made-Man and our Mediator, the finest example of a unifying reality, is a symbol which is refracted into a number of images (The Lamb, the Good Shepherd, etc.). Other symbols can be physical objects, such as the Cross, bread, or the steeple, but they can also very often be people, such as the three Persons of the Trinity, the Virgin Mary, the saints, priests, people in holy orders, and the laity. Symbols are made for mankind, for all of us, so that we can more clearly perceive the fullness and unity of love as expressed in Christ's last prayer on earth to his Father: "I have made your name known to them and will continue to make it known, so that the love with which you have loved me may be in them, and so that I may be in them." (Jn 17:26)

1. Cf. Le Gall. *Associés à l'œuvre de Dieu*, C.L.D. Chambray-lès-Tours, 1981, pp. 103-107.
2. "The Word became flesh, he lived among us" (Jn 1:14). For biblical quotations see the New Jerusalem Bible.

3. "That they may be one as we are one. With me in them and you in me, may they be so perfected in unity that the world will recognise that it was you who sent me and that you have loved them as you loved me." (Jn 17:22-23)
4. John Paul II, Encyclical Letter *Ut unum sint*, N°1
5. Constitution of the Sacred Liturgy, *Sacrosanctum Concilium*, published on December 4, 1963, N°66
6. John Paul II, Encyclical Letter *Ut unum sint*, N°66
7. The first and last books of the Bible.
8. Chapter two of the Dogmatic Constitution of the Church, *Lumen gentium*, deals with the People of God; chapter three was to follow later and is entitled: "The Hierarchical Constitution of the Church with special reference to the Episcopate."
9. Mt 16:18
10. Quoted in *Ut unum sint*, N°95

THE TRINITY

THE MYSTERY OF A SINGLE GOD IN
THREE BEINGS IS THE SOURCE OF ALL UNITY
AND ALL COMMUNION

THE FOREMOST SYMBOL OF CHRISTIANITY IS THAT OF THE HOLY TRINITY, ALTOGETHER AS ABSTRACT AS A MATHEMATICAL SIGN. THE Trinity designates the unity of three divine beings, the Father, the Son and the Holy Spirit, as a *triune*. From this word derives that mysterious and unfathomable equation 3=1 and 1=3. Although unique, God is indivisibly made up of three persons. The posing of this undemonstrable axiom, the beginning and the end of all things, explains nothing, and this notion of a triunal and absolute unity barely touches us.

The abstract Trinity is visually portrayed through the geometric symbol of an equilateral triangle which is often a feature at the top of baroque altar pieces. The three angles and the three sides are equal, but they constitute only a single surface. An eye is depicted in the centre of the triangle to show that God sees all—but this single eye, in its cyclopean force, does not so much suggest a look of love as that terrible conscience which pursues Victor Hugo's Cain.

The word "trinity" allows us to express the mystery of a single God in three beings. According to the three monotheistic religions of Judaism, Christianity and Islam, God can only be unique, for any multiplicity would be a sign of insufficiency or weakness. If there were several gods they would inevitably end up being antago-nists, as is demonstrated in Greek and Roman mythology. As the inheritor of Israel's monothe-ism, Christianity considers that a single God is nevertheless not solitary. First and foremost, Love exists within him and he spreads it throughout his creation. The mystery of God is a mystery of mutual love, of procreation. Our daily experience of life makes it easy for us to understand what a father is, or a son, or a sigh of love. As the origin of all things, God is not a being who is locked up inside himself, but is at the same time a Father full of tenderness, a Son who is the apple of his eye, and a Spirit of love which is a living link between them.

The Old Testament, which Jews and Christians alike venerate as the Word of God, already reveals this divine fatherhood. The prophet Hosea expressed it in these astonishing terms: "I myself taught Ephraim to walk, I myself took them by the arm, but they did not know that I was the one caring for them, that I was leading them with human ties, with leading-strings of love, that, with them, I was like someone lifting an infant to his cheek, and that I bent down to feed him" (Hos 11:3-4). Isaiah adds that this fatherly love also contains maternal tenderness: "Can a woman forget her baby at the breast, feel no pity for the child she has borne? Even if these were to forget, I shall not forget you" (Is 49:15).

The Trinitarian triangle surrounded by angels in the baptistry of the basilica of Santa Maria Maggiore in Rome.

His only Son came to reveal that Father full of tenderness, whose eternal love fills the New Testament.[1] It was first to Mary, the future mother of the Messiah, that the Archangel Gabriel revealed the mystery of a single God in three persons. The immaculate conception of the Son of the Almighty was to be the work of the third person of the Trinity, the Spirit of Love. The whole of the Trinity was expressed at the moment of the Annunciation.[2]

The Gospel according to Saint John defines the relationship between Christ and his Father, who are one. According to the divine plan, we should participate with the Spirit in that unity between Father and Son.[3] That is why Saint Paul's epistles are scattered with Trinitarian formulations, such as the following salutation: "The grace of the Lord Jesus Christ, the love of God and the fellowship of the Holy Spirit be with you all" (2 Cor 13:13).

We are baptized in the love that unites the three divine persons: that sacrament which is dispensed in the name of the Father, and of the Son, and of the Holy Spirit is recognized by all three Christian confessions (Catholic, Orthodox and Protestant). Love or friendship are emotions that we experience in our daily lives. They inspire in us a lasting communion with other people, but without causing a total fusion between individuals. As a guide towards divine love, the Trinity presents us with a perfect example of total communion, because its three persons are of one substance, and yet distinct.

There are numerous representations of the Trinity in Christian art. In contrast to Jews and Muslims who, in their infinite respect, refuse any depiction of God—this is the meaning of the commandment which Yahweh gave Moses on Mount Sinai[4]—Catholics and Orthodox Christians justify making images of God by the mystery of the Incarnation. Since one of the persons of the Trinity became man, it is then possible to depict him as a human in paintings or sculptures, and simple examples of this already appear in early Christianity. Similarly, the Holy Spirit, which manifested itself in the form of a dove, can be thus depicted. Nobody has ever seen the Father, the divine "source".

The oldest representation of the Trinity depicts the baptism of Christ: "And at once, as he was coming up out of the water, [Jesus] saw the heavens torn apart and the Spirit, like a dove, descending on him. And a voice came from heaven, 'You are my Son, the Beloved; my favour rests on you'." (Mk 1:10-12). The iconographic tradition depicts the hand of the Father emerging from the clouds to point out his Son, who already has the dove of the Spirit fluttering above him.

Much later, depicted as an old man with abundant hair, a bushy beard, and occasionally wearing a crown, a seated Father can be seen bearing up the Cross on which his Son has died, while the dove flutters between their two heads.

An episode in the story of Abraham was, from the days of the early Church, often used to evoke the mystery of the Trinity: the visit to him of three angels who are, in the biblical text, referred to alternately in the singular and plural (Gn 18:1-15), and in whom Christian tradition sees a prefiguration of the Trinity. As early as the

Trinitarian altar-piece in the abbey church of Paimpont (Ile-et-Vilaine, France). The dove of the Spirit hovers above the Son.

fifth century, this scene can be found among the mosaics of Santa Maria Maggiore in Rome, which were commissioned by Pope Sixtus III. It can also be seen in Ravenna. The monk Andrei Rublev's famous icon of the Trinity has become a familiar image, but it in fact depicts the visit of the three angels to Abraham. Their gazes are drawn in a circle, expressing their mutual love, and this circle is centred on a lamb, in the middle of the altar-table around which they are sitting. We too may enter into this circle of love through the sacrifice of the eucharist, which gives us access to that supreme love demonstrated by Christ the Saviour on the Cross.

The eucharistic prayer in fact finishes with a Trinitarian statement, which reveals all the meaning of the mystery of Christianity: "Through him Christ, with him, in him, in the unity of the Holy Spirit, all glory and honour is yours Almighty Father, for ever and ever." To which the entire congregation replies with a resounding Amen (in Hebrew "truly, assuredly").

1. "No one has ever seen God; it is the only Son, who is close to the Father's heart, who has made him known." (Jn 1:18)
2. "The Holy Spirit will come upon you, and the power of the Most High will cover you with its shadow. And so the child will be holy and will be called Son of God." (Lk 1:35)
3. Jn 17:20-21 (loc. cit.)
4. "You shall not make yourself a carved image or any likeness of anything in heaven above . . ." (Ex 20:4)

Giannicola di Paolo, The Baptism of Christ, *circa 1504.*
Louvre, Paris.

JESUS CHRIST

THE SON OF GOD BECAME MAN
TO SHARE OUR CONDITION AND ENABLE US TO
PARTICIPATE IN HIS DIVINITY

AS FAR AS HISTORIANS ARE CONCERNED, THERE IS NO DOUBT AS TO THE ACTUAL EXISTENCE OF JESUS. IT IS ATTESTED THAT HE lived two thousand years ago, at the beginning of our system of dating. He was crucified by order of Pontius Pilate and, during the following centuries, the faith which he inspired among his disciples was to become a determining factor in the history of the Roman Empire, and the rest of the western world. At the turn of the third millennium, this faith is still flourishing.

The Christian faith professes that Jesus is the Son of God, that he himself is God. As we have already pointed out, the divine plan is to bring about the salvation of mankind by offering us the chance to enter into communion with the three persons of the Trinity, the Father, the Son and the Holy Spirit. In order to allow us to participate in this mystery, it was necessary to create a living connection with us, and this was done through the Incarnation. One of the three became one of us, he came to share in our human condition so that we might dwell in their love. The mystery of the Trinity is, then, part of the mystery of the Incarnation: the Son of God became "the Son of Man."

This mystery is the inspiration behind some fundamental sections of the New Testament, and in particular the poetic prologue to the Gospel according to Saint John: "In the beginning was the Word: the Word was with God and the Word was God ... The Word became flesh, he lived among us, and we saw his glory ... No one has ever seen God; it is the only Son, who is close to the Father's heart, who has made him known" (Jn 1:1;14:18). The "Word", in its primary sense, here signifies the word conceived in the thought of God. This God born of God (*Credo*) was born in Bethlehem of the Virgin Mary, an event celebrated by the festival of Christmas.

The Son of God was announced under the name of Jesus—in Hebrew *Yehoshuah* or *Yeshuah*—which literally means "Yahweh has saved" or, more simply, "salvation". When the Angel of the Lord appears to Joseph in the first pages of the New Testament, he explains to him the essence of this mission of salvation.[1]

Jesus has been given the additional name of "Christ" which, in Greek, means "anointed" (*christos*) as it also does in the Hebrew "Messiah" (*mashiach*). The Christian tradition in fact recognizes his triple anointment as king, prophet and priest, which makes of him simultaneously the heir to King David and the great prophet whom Israel was awaiting (and whom the Jews are still awaiting today). The anointment which he received is that of the Holy Spirit, the Love which unites the persons of the Trinity, and

Giovanni Bellini, Christ Giving the Blessing.
Late fifteenth century. Louvre, Paris.

18

which was clearly expressed by the Father during his baptism in the Jordan.[2] When they are baptized, then confirmed, Christians also receive this anointment of the Holy Spirit and so become other christs, for Jesus was to be "the eldest of many brothers" (Rom 8:29).

Jesus can also be called Immanuel, which the Angel of the Lord we have already cited translates as "God-is-with-us".[3] Immanuel has, in the unity of his being, both divine and human nature "without confusion, without change, without division, without separation," according to the venerable phrase of the Council of Chalcedon. At once God and man, he becomes the mediator of a New Covenant, he is the "bridge" between heaven and earth. This is the true meaning of "pontiff" (in Latin *pontifex*, a "bridge-builder"). At the head of the priesthood, the Sovereign Pontiff represents the Priest-Christ in his role as a mediator, just as each bishop does in his diocese.

From this mystery of the Incarnation, conceived as an act of mediation, Christianity derives a full range of symbolism: a physical gesture such as the laying-on of hands, or earthly produce such as water, bread and wine, take on a spiritual dimension in the sacraments. By becoming man, Christ magnifies all of our images, since the depiction of God now becomes possible. The excesses caused by the creation of images even brought about a violent quarrel which led to the eigth-century movement of iconoclasm. The Second Council of Nicæa settled the question in 787 by the resolution that holy images were orthodox.

Both the West and the East have faithfully observed these commands. They have created a large cultural heritage of masterpieces depicting the Son of God as a man, from the Good Shepherd of the Catacombs to Rouault's Christ. Mosaics, frescoes, statues, paintings and Eastern icons have been produced by image-makers in prayer and fasting. Churches and museums teem with paintings of a highly religious inspiration. Only the Reformation of Calvin, for whom God was a spirit, forbade any decoration with such images on the bare, austere altars on which the sacred rite is celebrated. The Lutherans have adopted a more moderate position.

Jesus's divine humanity is perfectly expressed in the Transfiguration, which revealed his human face illuminated with divine glory before the apostles Peter, James and John. The Transfiguration was intended to strengthen their faith just at the moment when Christ was about to pass from this world to his Father's side by means of the Cross of Redemption. It lights up the disfigured face of the crucified Christ, who had sacrificed himself completely to the very end of his life on earth.[4]

1. "You must name him Jesus, because he is the one who is to save his people from their sins" (Mt 1:21). The identity of Jesus is abbreviated in the letters of the Greek word *ichthus* (fish): "Jesus Christ, Son of God, Saviour." This is why, in the catacombs, the fish is one of the symbols of Christ.
2. "This is my Son, the Beloved; my favour rests on him." (Mt 3:17)
3. Mt 1:23. Cf. also Is 7:14
4. "There in their presence he was transfigured: his face shone like the sun . . . " (Mt 17:2)

The Conquering Lamb, a symbol of Christ crucified and resurrected. Mosaic in the apse of Saint Clement's, Rome (twelfth century).

THE CROSS

THE CROSS ON WHICH JESUS DIED
FOR OUR SALVATION REMAINS A SIGN
OF COMPLETE SELF-SACRIFICE

IN ITS COMBINATION OF THE HORIZONTAL AND VERTICAL AXES, WHICH THUS EMBRACE THE WHOLE SYMBOLISM OF THE CARDINAL points, the cross has established itself in every culture and in all religions. The intersection of these two lines is a point of meeting, of convergence and of synthesis. Conversely, the cross also evokes images of torture, suffering and confrontation.

The Cross of Christ contains this dual symbolism, since it is at once the sacrificial altar which must reconcile mankind to itself and bring it nearer to God, and also the instrument of execution on which Jesus died. The cross is without doubt Christianity's most widespread and immediately recognized symbol: and we must now try to grapple with its true significance.

Jesus had come to earth with a mission of redemption and "went about doing good" (Acts 10:38), but he became a target for the jealousy of his nation's religious leaders, whose small-mindedness he protested against. The power of his preaching and the size of the movement which he had created made them plot against him, and they were to triumph at the moment of Easter. Pontius Pilate, the Roman Procurator of Judea, gave way in spite of himself under the Jews' pressure and condemned him to death for the capital offence of claiming to be the Son of God. But, for Christians, Jesus's death was not the end of his destiny. Christ was resurrected and

dwells at his Father's right hand. Like Moses and Jeremiah, Jesus had to bear the brunt of his people's refusal "by taking their guilt on himself" (Is 53:11) and, by his death and resurrection, fulfil Isaiah's prophecy: "Ill-treated and afflicted, he never opened his mouth, like a lamb led to the slaughter-house" (Is 53:7). Christ was not ignorant of this destiny, which was clearly stated from the beginning of the Gospels when John the Baptist presents Jesus as the Lamb of God.[1] He walked on knowingly towards his destiny and announced his imminent suffering and death on three occasions to his apostles.[2]

This "paschal" suffering by execution and death in fact obeys a mysterious necessity in the divine plan of salvation, as Jesus, when resurrected, explained to the disciples of Emmaus: "Was it not necessary that the Christ should suffer before entering into his glory?" (Lk 24:26). The humiliation which Christ suffered and the crucifixion are, for Saint John the Evangelist, nothing less than a royal investiture. Pilate asks him if he is a king, and the soldiers mock him by calling him "king of the Jews".[3] On Pilate's own orders,[4] and in latter-day representations, the cross carries a notice bearing four letters: I.N.R.I. (*Iesus Nazarenus Rex Iudeorum*), "Jesus the Nazarene, King of the Jews." The only way to understand Jesus's willing sacrifice is by seeing it as the supremely lucid expression of his love for us and

The Cross of Glory, symbol of death but a sign of life.

for his Father.[5] This love is such that the Son of God unreservedly submitted himself to the plan which the Father had made for our salvation. This is how he spoke before the Passion, in his last conversations with the apostles: "The prince of this world is on his way. He has no power over me, but the world must recognise that I love the Father and that I act just as the Father commanded." (Jn 14:30-31)

The Cross of Glory is, then, the ultimate revelation of perfect love. Its importance is explained to us by Jesus during the Last Supper, when he inaugurates the sacrament of the eucharist.[6] Some depictions of the crucifixion link it to the symbolism of the Trinity, in the same way which has been described for the baptism of Christ: a dove, symbolizing the Holy Spirit, hovers above the crucified figure. Indeed, the Son of God died as a man on the cross and "gave up his spirit" (Jn 19:30), that is to say that he communicated the Holy Spirit to us.

The water and the blood which flowed from his pierced side gave birth to the Church. A certain similarity can be seen here with the birth of Eve, whom God had shaped from Adam's rib.[7] The Church Fathers also say that the Cross is the nuptial bed on which the Church, the Bride of God, is impregnated by Christ the Bridegroom.[8]

The Cross is thus at the centre of the history of the Christian world. The motto of the Carthusian order is even: *Stat crux dum volvitur orbis*, "the Cross stands firm in the swirling of this world." That is why our universe is full of crosses. Most churches are built in the shape of a cross: the nave and the choir form the vertical axis, the transept (made up of two wings) the horizontal one. The fact that the choir is often off-centre can be explained by the way the crucified Christ's head leant to one side when he "gave up his spirit." Inside the church, the twelve crosses of consecration symbolize the "Apostles of the Lamb" (Rv 21:14). Christians often wear a cross around their necks, and the pectoral cross is the distinguishing mark of prelates. Christian tombs have, since antiquity, been marked by a cross.

The sign of the cross, which is used to give the blessing, joins the mystery of the Holy Trinity to the mystery of Redemption because, while tracing the cross, the names of the three persons are pronounced: "In the name of the Father [on the forehead], and of the Son [down to the waist] and of the Holy Spirit [from the left to the right shoulder, or the other way round for the Orthodox]. Amen." This symbolic progression summarizes life in its entirety, inspired by a love which carries on through to the end and which, going beyond our sufferings and our death, leads us to eternal life with Christ.

1. "The next day . . . [John] said, 'Look, there is the lamb of God that takes away the sin of the world'." (Jn 1:29)
2. Mt 16:21; 17:22-23; 20:18-19
3. Jn 18:33-37; 19:3-14
4. Jn 19:19
5. Jn 13:1
6. Mt 26:26-28
7. Jn 19:34 and Gn 2:21-24
8. Eph 5:25-27

Following pages: ivory crucifix in the abbey church of Paimpont (Ile-et-Vilaine). Seventeenth-eighteenth century.

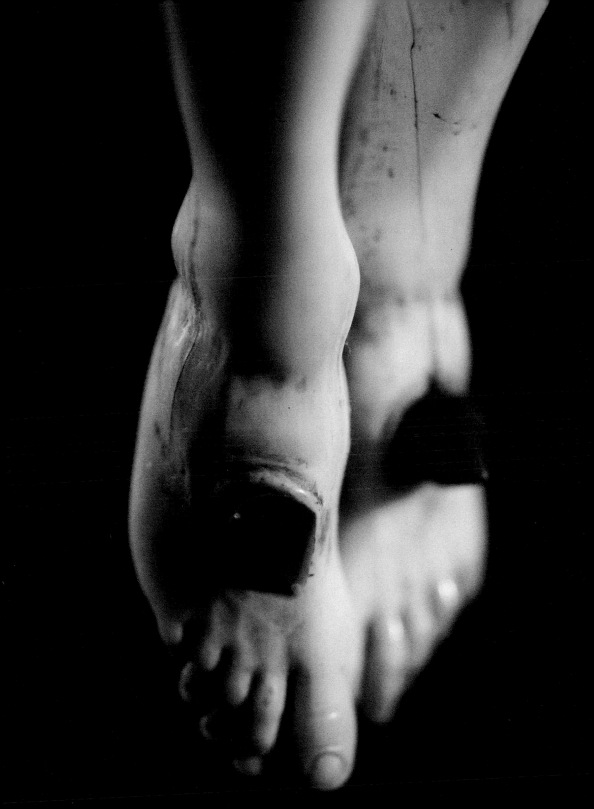

THE VIRGIN MARY

THE CONSECRATED IMAGE OF MATERNAL
TENDERNESS, THE MOTHER OF GOD DRAWS US STRAIGHT
TO THE HEART OF DIVINE LOVE

THE ARCHANGEL GABRIEL ANNOUNCED TO THE VIRGIN MARY THAT SHE WAS GOING TO CONCEIVE A SON, WHO WOULD BE THE descendant of David and whose reign would be everlasting. This designated him as the Messiah whom Israel had been awaiting. The Annunciation holds an important place in Europe's cultural heritage and has been painted on numerous occasions. The moment when Mary was summoned to become the Mother of the Saviour, and our Mother too, is the basis of her dignity.

We have already pointed out that the complete Trinity is presented to Mary in the announcement of Gabriel, who has been sent by the Father, as a messenger of the Incarnation of the Son, which will take place through the agency of the Holy Spirit. This divine plan of salvation mysteriously hangs on the agreement of a humble maiden from Nazareth. She gives it in her *Fiat*: "You see before you the Lord's servant, let it happen [in Latin, *fiat*] to me as you have said" (Lk 1:38).

Mary gives birth to the baby Jesus in Bethlehem. Forty days later, he is presented at the Temple of Jerusalem. Wise Men from the East come to worship him, then King Herod's jealousy forces the holy family to hide for a time in Egypt. After the king's death, Joseph, Mary and Jesus return to Nazareth where, for the next twenty years, Jesus grows up in obscurity.

Mary has a discreet role to play in the New Testament. Leaving aside the stories of Jesus's childhood in Matthew and Luke, what comes out most strongly is the important episode at the marriage feast in Cana where, following his mother's suggestion, he turns water into wine, the miracle which marks the beginning of his public life.[1] Mary is then seen again standing by the Cross. Just before dying, Jesus points out John, the "disciple whom he loved," and says to her: "Woman, this is your son." He then confirms this by saying to the disciple: "This is your mother."[2] The scene shows us that, when dying, Christ gave us his mother. Seven weeks later, while waiting for Pentecost, Mary is praying ardently with the apostles and is among them when the Holy Spirit comes down in the shape of tongues of fire.[3]

Mary is thus present at the essential moments of Jesus's birth, his death and the founding of the Church. The early councils of the undivided Church profess her discreet yet essential place in the plan of salvation. She is at the heart of the *Credo*, the profession of faith: "By the power of the Holy Spirit, he took flesh of the Virgin Mary and became man." Mary is not a female divinity. She is God's humble servant, but

Giovanni Sassoferrato, Virgin with Child and Saint John the Baptist. Seventeenth century. Louvre, Paris.

becomes his mother according to the nature of humanity. She provides Christ's human side, just as the Father provides his divine nature. It is then easy to understand how profound her relationship is with the Father and the Son, as well as with the Holy Spirit who impregnated her. Mary can be said to be the human revelation of God's maternal tenderness.

As the centuries passed, the devotion of the Catholics and the Orthodox to Mary continually increased. On the other hand, the Reformation considered that mankind's addresses to the Virgin—which were at times excessive and exclusive—were an offence to Christ's unique role as mediator. The Catholic Church believes that Mary has a maternal mediatory influence with her Son, and tradition dubs her *Omnipotentia supplex* ("the all-powerful suppliant"). The Dogmatic Constitution of the Church in the Second Vatican Council teaches that: "Mary's function as mother of men in no way obscures or diminishes this unique mediation of Christ, but rather shows its power" (N°60). Mary is the Mother of God and the Mother of the Church, but she is neither above God nor above the Church. "She is hailed as pre-eminent and as a wholly unique member of the Church" (N°53). In the image of the Mystical Body of Christ, she is not the Head, but the Neck, through which all her influence flows. The Church, the bride of God, is also a virgin and a mother.

The liturgical calendar shows the importance of Mary's place in Christian life. Following the chronological order of her life, her first festival is that of the Immaculate Conception, on December 8. This dogma, which was fixed by Pope Pius IX in 1854, professes that the Virgin was preserved from original sin in anticipation of the Redemption. Nine months later, on September 8, comes the Nativity of the Virgin; her presentation at the Temple is celebrated on November 21. March 25 (nine months before Christmas) is the Annunciation of the Lord to Mary. On May 31, the Visitation commemorates her welcome by her cousin Elizabeth. Each year, January 1 is the festival of Mary's divine Motherhood. The Presentation of the Lord at the Temple, or Candlemas, is on February 2. Our Lady of Dolours is celebrated on September 15 and her Assumption on August 15 (this dogma was established by Pope Pius XII in 1950). October 7 is the Feast of the Holy Rosary. Hardly a month goes by without there being a celebration of the Virgin Mary, leaving aside local festivals and countless pilgrimages of the Virgin.

The Rosary which has just been alluded to is a recitation of "Hail Marys" in fifteen decades, made up of five joyful, five sorrowful and five glorious mysteries. It is known as the "poor man's psalter": the number of prayers thus pronounced—150—being the same as the number of psalms. By means of a humble repetitive prayer, which can be found in all religions (such as the Orthodox "Prayer of Jesus"), the Rosary enables us to enter alongside Mary into the mystery of salvation.

1. Jn 2:1-12
2. Jn 1:26-27
3. Acts 1:14; 2:1-4

Virgin of Jeanne d'Evreux. Fourteenth century.
Louvre, Paris.

THE CHURCH

THE CHURCH IS THE ASSEMBLY
OF THE PEOPLE OF GOD SERVED BY THE BISHOPS,
PRIESTS AND DEACONS

THE CHURCH IS OFTEN CONSIDERED TO BE AN INSTITUTION WHICH IS AT ONCE SOLID AND FRAGILE, FIRM AND OVERBEARING, WHOSE religious and moral demands are excessive or outdated. Throughout history, the Church and Churches have experienced tensions, schisms and scandals. The mystery of the Church lies elsewhere. As the Latin and Greek word *ecclesia* suggests, it is an "assembly" which has been called together (from the Greek verb *ek-kaleein*). The first of these "assemblies", which marked the birth of the People of God, took place on Mount Sinai after the escape from Egypt.[1] It consists in a liturgy of Covenant, from the Greek *leitourgia*, which originally meant any service given to the community by one or several of its members. In this case it is first God who "serves" his people, even before they "serve" him. The liturgy is the work of God and of his people, which is renewed in the New Testament with the mystery of Pentecost.

The first symbolic reality of Christianity is the Trinity; we shall be returning to this fundamental element throughout this book. Now, the Church's true identity is in the union of the faithful tied up with the mystery of the Trinity as defined by Saint Irenæus, bishop of Lyons and second-century martyr: "Hence the universal Church is to be a people brought into unity from the unity of the Father, the Son and the Holy Spirit."[2] Churches are places where the Church comes together. In architectural splendour, hewn stones must receive living ones.

The People of God take the primary place in the Church. They are the Bride of God summoned to join herself with her God, depicted throughout the Bible and *The Song of Songs*. According to the New Testament, the Groom of this Bride is the incarnated Son, whose wedding day has been prepared for him by the Father.[3] In the Book of Revelation, this image is linked to that of the City.[4] Quite the opposite of the Tower of Babel, the builders of which wished to unite themselves against God and violate his kingdom, the Church is a gift of God which comes down from heaven, and thus is "a sign and instrument, that is, of community with God and of unity among all men" (*Lumen gentium*, N°1).

To this nuptial image, Saint Paul adds the image of the Mystical Body of Christ: he is the head and we are the members.[5] This is where it becomes necessary to organize the People of God, so that each person should play his part, like the members of a body, and the hierarchy of the bishops grouped around the Pope is at its service. "For you, I am a bishop; with you, I am a Christian," said Augustine to the faithful of Hippo. These two complementary symbols affirm how profound the unity is which exists between Christ and the

Romanesque church at Orcival (Puy-de-Dôme, France);
its steeple unifies the village in its upward thrust to heaven.

Church. This nuptial mystery makes the assembly of Christians into "the Full Son", the temple of the Holy Spirit, begotten of the Father, whom they invoke as *Abba* ("papa" in Armenian).

Christ entrusted his Church to Saint Peter. Despite the persecutions of the early Christians in the Roman Empire, Saint Peter carried out his mission by going to Rome and living there until he too was martyred. This is why Saint Peter is considered to be the first Bishop of Rome, and his successors bore the same title. When the Emperor Constantine was himself converted to Christianity (312-313) and the Bishop of Rome started to exercise his ministry in S. Giovanni in Laterano, Saint Peter's tomb in the Vatican's necropolis began to be venerated, and a magnificent basilica soon rose there, which has been enriched throughout the centuries. The Council of Chalcedon (450-451) consecrated the primacy of the Bishop of Rome and entrusted him with the mission of attending to the unity of the Church, thus making the capital of the Western Empire, badly shaken by barbarian invasions, into the capital of the Christian world.

Christians, however, have not been able to avoid some painful separations. Since 1054, the Orthodox Churches have been independent of Rome, even though their faith and spiritual practices are virtually identical. The Churches created by the Reformation of Luther and Calvin have moved even further away from the Catholic Church. As the third millennium approaches, Pope John Paul II launched an appeal for church unity through a commitment to ecumenism in his encyclical of May 25, 1995. Leading by example,

he asks us to confess what separates us from unity, to intensify our dialogues and prayers, and even now to live out the unity of all who believe in Jesus Christ.

The adjective "catholic" expresses the Church's universal vocation, for "universal" is precisely what it means in Greek (*katholikos*, from *kath-holou*: "according to all"). The article of the *Credo* which deals with the Church clearly states this demand for unity: "We believe in one, holy, catholic and apostolic Church." Ecumenism aims to recover this universal mystery of the Church, since the Greek word *oikoumene* means "the inhabited world" (from *oikos*, "house") and, by extension, the entirety of the known universe.

The churches in our towns and villages symbolize the unity of the human community. Their steeples, which point up towards heaven, display our common upward desire for God. The East prefers cupolas, which symbolize the protective heavenly vault and, even more, God's tenderness which envelops us.

1. "Yahweh gave me the two stone tablets inscribed by the finger of God, exactly corresponding to what Yahweh had said to you on the mountain, from the heart of the fire, on the day of the Assembly." (Dt 9:10)
2. Quoted at the beginning of the Dogmatic Constitution of the Church in the Second Vatican Council (N°4).
3. "The kingdom of Heaven may be compared to a king who gave a feast for his son's wedding." (Mt 22:2)
4. "I saw the holy city, the new Jerusalem, coming down out of heaven from God, prepared as a bride dressed for her husband." (Rv 21:2)
5. 1 Cor 12:12-26

A chapel in the cloister of the basilica of Sainte-Anne d'Auray (Morbihan, France); it is rich in simple symbols: cross, tabernacle, altar and pulpit.

THE ANGELS

ANGELS WERE PRESENT AT EACH
SIGNIFICANT MOMENT IN THE LIFE OF CHRIST. THEY ARE OUR
COMPANIONS AND OUR GUARDIANS

ON THE CEILINGS OF BAROQUE CHURCHES THERE IS AN ABUNDANCE OF PLUMP CHERUBIM WITH GOLDEN WINGS. IN TWO, OR often three, dimensions they escort Christ, the Virgin or the saints, or else are positioned around the edges of the clouds. But are these angels anything more than just pious decoration? For many of our contemporaries, they are a pleasantly imagistic expression of inaccessible perfection, or simply of an escape into unreality. They are the inhabitants of some imaginary "seventh heaven".

But the liturgy, as well as Holy Scripture, talks constantly of angels and makes them into discreet, yet efficient, participants in the story of salvation, messengers of God and mankind's companions. In Greek, the word angel literally means "ambassador" or "messenger". Angels are the witnesses of God's tender attentions to us. As such, they are our guardian angels.

In the Gospels, angels are always present at the key moments of the mystery of Jesus Christ. The Annunciation is probably the best-known scene in which an angel plays a part.[1] At Christ's birth, "a great throng of the hosts of heaven" greets him by singing God's praises.[2] After the temptation in the wilderness, angels "looked after him"[3] and, at the moment of the agony in Gethsemane, "an angel . . . coming from heaven" comforted him.[4] On Easter morning, two angels announce the news that Jesus has risen to the holy women,[5] and when Jesus ascends to heaven, they are once more there to reassure the apostles that he will return.[6]

Following the example of Christ's life, the entirety of the liturgy is accompanied by angels, who are the perfect singers of God's glory. The "Glory to God" of festive days is sung in unison with the angelic choir at Bethlehem. During the mass, we are asked to join our voices to their song of praise by chanting "Holy, Holy, Holy."[7] The angels are part of that "invisible world" which is mentioned in the first article of the *Credo*.

Thus we approach "Mount Zion and the city of the living God, the heavenly Jerusalem where the millions of angels have gathered for the festival" (Heb 12:22). We must love the angels, sing praises with them[8] and pray to them. They are faithful, efficient friends who allow us to understand, like Saint-Exupéry's fox, that "the essential is invisible to our eyes."

1. Lk 1:26-38
2. Lk 2:13
3. Mk 1:13
4. Lk 22:43
5. Mt 28:2-7
6. Acts 1:10-11
7. Is 6:3; Rv 4:8
8. Ps 138:1

Preceding double page: basilica of Saint Peter in Rome, its square and the Pope's apartments seen from Bernini's colonnade.
Opposite: angel in the church of Saint Alexius on the Aventine in Rome.

THE SAINTS

AFTER A LIFE ON EARTH DEVOTED
TO THE SERVICE OF GOD, SAINTS ARE AN EXAMPLE
TO US AND ALSO PROTECT US

BOTH THE TIME AND THE SPACE WE LIVE IN ARE FULL OF SAINTS. FROM ST. PETERSBURG TO SANTIAGO DE COMPESTELLA, FROM St. Ives in Cornwall to St. Peter in Minnesota, our world is littered with towns and villages named after saints. If, in the early days of Christianity, Saint Paul called all the believers in Christ "saints" or "holy people",[1] this title has, since the eleventh century, been reserved for those whom the Holy See has canonized, and who are venerated by the Church. At the time, it was absolutely necessary to regulate the occasionally excessive worship which, since the Roman persecutions, had been accorded to martyrs, as well as all Christians who had displayed outstanding virtue. The custom was to celebrate the day on which they died, or on which their relics were transported, and the tradition still continues today with the calendar of Saints' days.

The procedure of beatification, then of canonization, was defined by Pope Alexander III in the twelfth century, and it has been revised on numerous occasions since. It calls on the authority of the Church to declare that a given person has entered into the Glory of God and should be venerated as a saint. An investigation is carried out, followed by a "trial" which includes several adversarial exchanges between the promoter of the cause (for) and the Devil's advocate (against).

After the Virgin Mary, whose vital place in the Church we have already discussed, the saints include apostles and martyrs, a few Popes and prelates, clerics of all ranks and some lay people. A saint is someone who, guided by the Holy Spirit, has consecrated his or her life to God and to others. They lend their names to parishes and monasteries, and each of us receives a name at baptism which puts us under the protection of a given "patron" saint. Saints are generally depicted with their heads surrounded by a halo, which symbolizes God's Holiness radiating from them. Since the days of the Old Testament, men like Moses and Elijah have been transfigured by the light of God; that is why they stood alongside Christ on Mount Tabor.[2]

But the worship which we give to Saints in no way reduces the worship we first owe to God and to Christ. As the Preface of Saints' Feasts puts it: "You are glorified in your saints, for their glory is the crowning of your gifts." Worship of relics has also been part of the Catholic tradition since earliest times. This is perfectly consistent with the mystery of Incarnation which respects the body, the members of Christ, and the temple of the Holy Spirit.[3]

1. 2 Cor 1:1
2. Ex 34:29; 2 Kgs 2:11; Mt 17:3
3. 1 Cor 6:15-19

Saint John the Evangelist, ivory book cover.
Tenth century. Louvre, Paris.

BAPTISM

AS AN INITIATION INTO CHRISTIAN LIFE, BAPTISM IS A SECOND BIRTH INTO THE CHURCH

BAPTISM IS THE FIRST OF THE SACRAMENTS, OR "SACRED ACTS", WHICH ARE BOTH VISIBLE SIGNS AND INSTRUMENTS OF INVISIBLE grace. They are symbols in the true sense of the word: by means of concrete gestures they bring about spiritual effects, uniting mankind with God through the interaction of body and soul.

The sacraments are an essential part of Catholicism and are derived from the mystery of the redeeming Incarnation. This close link between words (the "form") and material elements (the "matter") allows the Church to carry on its mission of salvation, through the Son of God who became man. It is necessary to make a distinction between his humanity, which provides an "espousing" instrument of our salvation, and sacraments which are "discrete" from him. But the governing symbolism of both is of the same nature. Sacraments perpetuate and personalize Christ's redemptive mission and are accessible to all those who wish to enter into their mystery.

The Church itself can be considered to be the "Original Sacrament." The seven sacraments take their source from here as the main channels of divine grace, having been instituted more or less clearly by Christ and attested in the New Testament. They are baptism, confirmation, the mass, holy orders, matrimony, penance and the anointing of the sick. These sacred acts are present throughout a believer's life, and are the outward signs of his religious commitment until the last moments of his earthly life.

Baptism (from the Greek verb *bapto* or *baptizo*, "to plunge") effectively "plunges" the believer into the mystery of the Trinity, into the mystery of the death and resurrection of Christ, and into the community of the Church. The most significant form of baptism is by triple immersion, associated with the words: "I baptize you in the name of the Father and of the Son and of the Holy Spirit." But it is most frequently administered by ablution: water is poured onto the head of the person being baptized. In accordance with ancient traditions, Catholics generally baptize young children, in preparation for a religious upbringing, but an increasingly large number of adult believers are also baptized.

Born again of water and of the Spirit,[1] the baptized believer enters into the Mystical Body of Christ thus becoming, according to Saint Paul, one of its living members,[2] one of the "heirs of God" (Rm 8:17). He is called upon to grow up in the Christian faith, and the other sacraments will mark the various stages of this growth.

1. Jn 3:5
2. "For as with the human body which is a unity although it has many parts—all the parts of the body, though many, still making up one single body—so it is with Christ." (1 Cor 12:12)

Font in Saint-Cornély church in Carnac (Morbihan, France).

CONFIRMATION

THE GIFT OF THE SPIRIT, THROUGH THE APPLICATION OF HOLY OIL, TURNS A BAPTIZED BELIEVER INTO AN ADULT IN THE FAITH

CONFIRMATION COMPLETES AND PERFECTS WHAT BAPTISM BEGAN. IN SIMPLE TERMS, IT IS THE SACRAMENT OF GROWING INTO A mature Christian. A young believer could well remain a "child" and never become a "grown Christian", just as we talk of a "grown man", if he didn't receive the gift of the Spirit during this ceremony, which more strongly "confirms" his existence in Christ.

In order to receive the sacrament of confirmation, an adolescent has already publicly and willingly professed the faith which he has received from his family (and which, from the age of reason onwards, can be celebrated in a private eucharist). That is why the expression "profession of faith" is extremely fitting. Customs differ widely between countries: in France, for example, there is the "solemn communion" and believers can be confirmed before making their profession of faith. Whatever the practice, confirmation plays the same indispensable part in our lives as the Pentecost, which brought an end to the mystery of Easter and allowed the apostles to go forth and bear witness to their faith.

The most important part of the confirmation ceremony is a light anointment with chrism, a holy oil which is consecrated by the bishop and the priests on Maundy Thursday. It penetrates the believer's forehead and symbolizes the Spirit, which must from now on be the guiding force behind everything he does. At the same time, the celebrant (generally a bishop, who can be accompanied by priests or can delegate to them) pronounces these words: "[Name], be sealed with the Gift of the Holy Spirit," and the confirmand replies: "Amen". He is from that moment a fully fledged member of the People of God, a "layman" (from the Greek *laos*, "people").

The anointment is also a symbol of the strength which the Spirit gives. Chrism is similar to the oil which was used for massaging wrestlers' muscles to make them suppler for the fight and more difficult to grapple with.

Baptism, confirmation and the taking of holy orders stamp a "character" on the soul, that is to say an indelible spiritual mark which allows different degrees of access to the Christian religion. That is why they are received only once, as opposed to the others which can be repeated.

The three sacraments of baptism, confirmation and the eucharist bring about "Christian initiation." In the early ages of Christianity, they were received together during a single ceremony (the Easter vigil was the most popular time for this), which introduced the "neophyte" ("new plant" in Greek) into the "divine" mysteries. This sequence is still followed today when an adult is baptized.

The gesture of the sacrament of confirmation: anointment with holy chrism on the forehead.

MASS

THE EUCHARIST IS THE RENEWAL OF CHRIST'S
SACRIFICE AND, THROUGH THE COMMUNION, GIVES US
ACCESS TO THE MYSTERY OF SALVATION

THROUGH THE AGES, THE MASS HAS PERPETU-
ATED THE UNIQUE SACRIFICE OF THE SON OF
GOD WHICH, AS WE HAVE EXPLAINED, IS
the key to our Redemption. It is a pacific offering
which makes Christ's sacrifice a present reality, and
it is at the heart of the Christian life. It consists of
a spoken liturgy, along with songs, prayers and several readings from the Bible, and a eucharistic
liturgy during which the bread and the wine are
transformed on the altar (or "transubstantiated")
into the body and blood of Christ.

It was in anticipation of the sacrifice of the
New Covenant that, on the eve of his death,
Christ wished to celebrate the Jewish Passover
with his disciples.[1] With them, he then followed
the normal ritual of the passover meal. The
Christian Mass has adopted many Jewish prayers
and practices, notably the blessings (*berakoth*) of
the table, which are the origin of the eucharistic
prayers, and reinterpreted them.

Since, according to tradition, the head of
the passover meal had to make a speech explain-
ing the meaning of the ritual, while the paschal-
lamb was being served, which commemorated the
escape from Egypt, so Jesus explains to his disciples that he is the true Paschal-Lamb, he that
"takes away the sin of the world."[2] At the
moment when the main meal was begun, the
head pronounced a blessing (in Greek *eucharistia*,

"act of grace") over the unleavened bread. That is
why Jesus consecrates it by presenting it as his
body: "This is my body given for you" (Lk 22:19).
At the end of the meal a fourth cup of wine was
normally blessed, so Christ too consecrates the
wine, making it into his own blood: "This cup is
the new covenant in my blood poured out for
you." He then adds, "Do this in remembrance of
me"(*ibid*). This ritual of remembrance of Israel
goes further than a simple commemoration. It
brings the past into the present and even antici-
pates the future: it is as if these three temporal
dimensions were telescoped into one another.
When partaking of the eucharist, Christians
become contemporaries of the Crucifixion in the
present of the Church, according to a ritual
which will last "until he [the Lord] comes" (1 Cor
11:26). Ordination allows a priest to consecrate
the bread and the wine and, by so doing, he effectively renews Christ's sacrifice, just as Jesus antici-
pated it on the eve of the Passion.

The Catholic faith professes that the bread
really becomes Jesus's body and the wine his
blood. In this way, at the table of the Last Supper
and on our altars, Jesus is actually present in the
symbolic and sacramental state of a sacrificial victim, whose body and blood have been separated.
This brings us face to face with the entire mystery
of our Redemption, since these tangible elements

During the procession at the beginning of the mass, the deacon,
wearing a dalmatic, solemnly carries an adorned evangelistary.

46

put the living, glorious Christ within our reach. At the end of the eucharistic prayer, the congregation of the faithful gives its assent to the mystery of the Covenant, which has been renewed on the altar, with a solemn "Amen". The Lord's Prayer can then be recited. This is the prayer of children reconciled to their Father through the sacrifice of his Son, who became man. The ritual of peace-giving then follows, manifesting the reconciliation of the brethren to one another.

The congregation then communes with this sacrifice at the eucharistic table. When, respecting the pre-ordained steps, we receive the body and the blood of Christ, we gradually enter into close communion with the Son: "As the living Father sent me and I draw life from the Father, so whoever eats me will also draw life from me" (Jn 6:57). United to Jesus Christ, Christians can, through him, participate in the very unity of the Trinity itself.

Thus, of all the sacraments, the eucharist is essential for the Church. According to an expression handed down by tradition: "The Church makes the Eucharist; the Eucharist makes the Church." Through the ministry of the priests, the eucharist is a celebration of that unique sacrifice in all places and for a variety of different communities and religious assemblies. This celebration, which is a concentrated version of what God has done for us and what he continues to do, creates and maintains Church unity.

Accordingly, the faithful should take part in the Sunday Mass, for that was the day on which the Lord was resurrected. During the communion,

a member of the Mystical Body of Christ is guaranteed "to receive that which he is," to quote one of Saint Augustine's telling phrases. Furthermore, it is highly recommended for priests to celebrate mass every day, and for the faithful to partake of it if they can. The office of eucharist is also part of the daily routine for monks and nuns. Fervent Christians can repeat word for word what one of the martyrs of Abitena (Tunisia) said in February of the year 304: "We cannot live without the Lord's Meal."

An extremely ancient Church tradition accepts the offerings of the faithful, who ask the officiating priest to present their wishes at the altar during the course of the mass. This practice should by no means be interpreted as a pricing of the sacraments, administration of which for money (simony) was vigorously forbidden by the Holy See on numerous occasions during the Middle Ages and by the Council of Trent. The mass is priceless and its universal implications surpass any personal intention. It is simply a matter of honouring the ministry of the priest who agrees to offer up a mass for a particular reason (one honorarium per mass is authorized).

1. "And he said to them, 'I have ardently longed to eat this Passover with you before I suffer'." (Lk 22:15)
2. He that was announced by John the Baptist, Jn 1:29-36.

Preceding double page: Papal mass at the basilica of Saint Peter in Rome, December 14, 1995. Opposite: basilica Santa Maria Maggiore in Rome: the altar servers are dressed in soutanes and surplices.

HOLY ORDERS

THE SACRAMENT OF HOLY ORDERS CONSECRATES THOSE WHO HAVE BEEN CALLED TO TRANSMIT THE GIFTS OF GOD TO THE SERVICE OF THEIR BROTHERS

TO GUARANTEE THE LASTING AUTHENTICITY OF THE COMMUNION OF LOVE WHICH PROCEEDS FROM HIS MYSTICAL BODY, CHRIST himself provided it with living signs of his presence and his deeds. After the Resurrection, he appeared to his apostles and gave them a mission to convert the nations:[1] they are thus vital witnesses of his humanity, while the gift of the Holy Spirit at Pentecost fills them with power from on high.[2]

Among these apostles was Simon, called Peter, whom Jesus designated as the foundation of his Church, even mysteriously identifying himself with him as the payer of the religious tax of the shekel.[3] This simple, generous man, originally a fisherman from Galilea, experienced a moment of weakness by denying Christ three times over during the night of the Passion. But having received three declarations of love from him, the Risen Lord nevertheless chose him to watch over his entire flock.[4]

Thus, by the will of Christ, his Church, which is a living body, was structured by Peter and the Apostles. In turn, they transmitted to the chosen, by the laying-on of hands, the dignity of being Christ's representatives, with the strength of the Holy Spirit which they needed. Throughout the centuries, this mission has continued in the ministry of bishops, to whom the plenitude of the sacrament of Holy Orders has given the status of being the apostles' successors.

They are Christ's signs and instruments in each of their dioceses and their churches. Saint Augustine considered himself to be both a member of the Church, like the faithful of Hippo, as well as their living sign of the Lord, invested with the power to unite them in him. In the same way, the Second Vatican Council's Constitution of the Church presents God's People first and foremost, before specifying the Church's hierarchy based on the episcopate.

The bishops are subordinates of the Bishop of Rome, Peter's successor, who presides over the Church's mission. "The Servant of the Servants of God," the Vicar of Christ, he is the only one to receive the honorific title of "pope" (from the Greek *pappas*, a child's word for "father"). As a sign and reference of its unity, he is one of the Catholic Church's main symbols. He is generally assisted in his curia and unites the college of bishops around him for councils and synods. For the faithful of each diocese, the bishop fulfils the role of a pastor, of a priest and of a doctor, and hence participates in Christ the Lord's own ministry. From the earliest Church onwards, he has been assisted by priests whom he ordains and who share his ministry; who, like him, can administer the eucharist acting *in persona Christi* ("in the person of Christ"). He is also aided by deacons (from the Greek *diakonos*, "servant"), to whom he gives

Ordination of priests: the ordinand prostrates himself during the singing of the litany of the saints.

a participation in the Order, not in the ministry itself but for certain sacramental "services". The diaconate had long been a preparation for the priesthood and has, since the Second Vatican Council, become a permanent order once more.

Bishops, priests and deacons thus represent the three levels of the sacrament of Holy Orders, which is conferred by the laying of hands on the head of the ordinand and then by the prayer of ordination. Bishops are the only ministers (in the Latin sense of the term *minister*, "servant") of ordination. But, during the ordination of priests, any priests present also lay on their hands. Anointment of the head for bishops and of the hands for priests are complementary rituals. Bishops are given their pontifical insignia, the mitre and the crook; the priests receive a stole and a chasuble, as well as the bread and wine for the mass; deacons are presented with the book of the Gospels, before being clothed in a stole and a dalmatic. When not officiating at ceremonies at which the ecclesiastics have to wear their liturgical vestments (which will be explained further on), their official dress is a black soutane tightened round the waist by a wide belt, or, since 1963, what is called the "clergyman": a black or grey suit with a small cross on its lapel, over a dark shirt decked with a white dog-collar.

The Pope is the only one to wear a white soutane; a white cape covers his shoulders and chest. On his finger, he wears "The Fisherman's Ring", in memory of Saint Peter's origins, which was used for sealing letters (*sub annulo piscatoris*). On his head, he wears a white calotte and round his neck a pectoral cross, hanging from a chain.

The Cardinals—Bishops who are closer to the Pope—first exercised their ministry in the different quarters of Rome (in Latin *cardines*) and they constitute a sort of pontifical senate. They receive a red biretta (a type of square cap) and are entirely dressed in red (soutane, cape and calotte); they wear a ring on their fingers and their pectoral crosses hang from a red cord. The colour red (also called "cardinal's scarlet") symbolizes the fidelity which they pledge to the Pope, going as far as to shed their blood for Christ and his Church. The Bishops' and Archbishops' colour is violet (soutane, cape and calotte); they also wear a ring which symbolizes their marriage to the Church (they constitute the sacrament of "Christ the bridegroom"); their pectoral cross hangs from a green cord (violet during Advent and Lent). Certain other ecclesiastical dignitaries, such as the protonotaries apostolical, also wear violet vestments.

RELIGIOUS PROFESSION

The expression "to take holy orders" is well known, though it does not actually mean the taking of the sacrament of Holy Orders, but corresponds to the choice of making a religious profession. Apart from the "secular" clergy, so called because they administer the sacraments to the *sæcularia* (that is to say, to the faithful of the People of God in "this world"), the Church also includes what are called "regular" orders, because their members are committed to obeying *regula* (written rules governing their lives). The men and women belonging to these orders are not part of the hierarchy we have just described, even if

Two cardinals in ceremonial dress: their pectoral crosses hang from red and golden cords.

some of them do become bishops, priests or deacons (they even include several Popes), but are living symbols of the holiness of the Church.[5]

Religious life is not a sacrament, but a state of consecration to God, which is prepared for by a noviciate: before the Church, which is to receive them in the name of God, the candidate professes perpetual vows of poverty, chastity and obedience (and other vows appertaining to certain religious communities), which are known as religious vows.

This is a spontaneous act, a "promise made to God" according to Saint Thomas Aquinas, a lifelong commitment to the path of perfection. Baptism has made the Christian a son of God, and Confirmation has invested him with the Holy Spirit; here he is called to holiness, that is to say he must become absolutely open to the inward movements of the Spirit of Love. From this personal, intimate reaching out on the part of all Christians evolves the purity of the entire Christian community, that divine Bride whom Saint Paul calls "holy and faultless" (Ep 5:27).

The grace of God inspires a particular calling in those men and women who have left everything to follow him, leading many disciples with them and, above and beyond anything else, the People of God. Such is the origin of monastic and religious orders, which are successors to the early Church's communities of hermits. There are contemplative orders, often inspired by the Rule of Saint Benedict, including the Benedictines, the Cistercians and the Carthusians. Later on came other orders which mingle prayer with a variety of apostolic works: the Dominicans (from Saint Dominic), the Franciscans and the Poor Clares (from Saints Francis and Clare of Assisi), the White Friars and the Carmelites (reformed by Saint John of the Cross and Saint Theresa of Avila). Other charitable or teaching orders are still being created today.

The superiors of abbeys of monks are called Father Abbots, which is to say "father" twice over, since *abba* in Armenian means "papa". Abbots wear the ring and the pectoral cross (with a green or violet cord), but they are dressed in cowled robes, which are black for Benedictines and white for Cistercians ("black friars" and "white friars"). The rule of prayer and of joyful self-denial, which those in orders have chosen in order to live their faith out to the full, reminds all baptized Christians that they, too, should "prefer nothing to the love of Christ," as the rule of Saint Benedict demands.[6]

1. "Go, therefore, make disciples of all nations; baptise them in the name of the Father and of the Son and of the Holy Spirit." (Mt 28:19)
2. Acts 1:8
3. "You are Peter and on this rock I will build my community." (Mt 16:18) Cf. also Mt 17:27 for the shekel.
4. "Jesus said to him, 'Feed my lambs'." (Jn 21:15-17)
5. Dogmatic Constitution of the Church in the Second Vatican Council, N°44
6. "No one who prefers father or mother to me is worthy of me. No one who prefers son or daughter to me is worthy of me." (Mt 10:37)

Preceding pages: left, a Franciscan wearing his habit; right, Cardinal Paul Poupard.
Opposite: a Missionary Sister of Charity (of Mother Theresa).

MATRIMONY

THE CELEBRATION OF MARRIAGE
DIGNIFIES WITH DIVINE LOVE THE SOLEMN
UNDERTAKING MADE BY THE SPOUSES

THE REQUIREMENTS OF CATHOLIC MARRIAGE ARE BASED ON THE FUNDAMENTAL PRINCIPLES OF UNITY AND INDISSOLUBILITY, TOGETHER with a commitment to the bearing of children. The changes in contemporary society, in a world in which the importance of spirituality is decreasing, make such a doctrine difficult to accept. This phenomenon seems to manifest itself in the fragility and instability of modern society, and people can quite often suffer disastrous effects from it in their private lives. In this way, the Church's message is often misunderstood, while what it tries to do is to serve the honour of God as well as the dignity of mankind.

All religions have, in one way or another, made the conjugal union sacred, for the mystery of life and of child-bearing generally inspires a sense of divinity. As a reaction against pagan practices, which were often degrading, the Judaeo-Christian Revelation gives matrimony a powerful symbolic dimension, for one of the most important currents that run through the Bible is that of the marriage between God and his People.

From the moment of their creation, a man and a woman, united in life, form together an image of God; the man leaves his father and his mother to join himself with his wife, and they become one flesh.[1] Moses went to Egypt to fetch the People of God, like a fiancée, and lead them through the desert to Sinai, the mountain of their nuptial Covenant with Yahweh. The *Song of Songs* chants the mutual love of Yahweh and Israel. Finally, the New Testament reveals that Jesus is the Bridegroom of the new People of God, the Church.

Christian matrimony is the sacramental sign of that union between Christ and his Church. According to the teaching of Saint Paul: "This mystery has great significance, but I am applying it to Christ and the Church" (Ep 5:32). The spouses who exchange their vows before God and in front of the priest who represents him—and who blesses the couple in his role as a sacramental witness, according to the ancient rules which were codified in the sixteenth century by the Council of Trent—participate in the fullness of this holy unity.

The spouses are said to give themselves the sacrament of matrimony; indeed, their mutual "yes" given one to the other in their human love is the sign and instrument of that very love which God bears for them. Those that live out the joy and depth of love realize that the force which moves them also inspires them: it comes from outside them and leads them to excel themselves. For them it can be a true revelation of divine love, which nourishes their mutual feeling and guarantees its permanence.

1. Gn 1:27; 2:24.

Wedding rings.

PENANCE

DISTANCED FROM GOD BY SIN,
THE PENITENT FINDS THE PEACE HE IS LOOKING FOR IN
REPENTANCE AND ABSOLUTION

THROUGHOUT HISTORY, MAN HAS REALIZED THAT HE IS SINFUL. WHILE HE ASPIRES TO THE UNTAINTED LIFE WHICH DIVINE TEACHING shows is available to him, he is subjected to numerous and various temptations and sometimes succumbs to them. All religions, therefore, have their rites of purification: ablutions, baptisms, or even public penance which can, at times, take aberrant forms.

As far as the Catholic faith is concerned, there exists an original sin, which is explained in allegorical terms in the opening pages of the Bible. In his Incarnation as the Redeemer (from the Latin *redimere*, "to buy back", notably to pay a captive's ransom and give him back his freedom), Jesus Christ came to deliver us. But a principle of evil is at work in this world,[1] that "devil" who divides us. The world and its history—that of this century which is coming to a close, for example—clearly show how perverse mankind can be, and how this perversion makes us suffer.

Baptism washes away original sin, and penance (or reconciliation) cleanses us of later personal faults. In the Gospels, Christ affirms, while curing the paralysed man, that he has the divine privilege of forgiving sins.[2] On the evening of his Resurrection, this power was transferred to the apostles[3] and, beyond the apostles, to those whom they have chosen to continue their work. Before his sins are forgiven, the sinner must make an act of contrition, that is, to express regret for having committed them. He then specifies the nature of his sins by confessing them to a priest, who gives him absolution, on the condition of a symbolic satisfaction, which generally takes the form of a few prayers. Contrition, confession and satisfaction are the necessary steps to obtaining absolution.

The Church invites its faithful to receive this sacrament at least once a year, at Easter. "Doing one's Easter duty" consists in confession and communion. As in our daily lives, so in the life of the spirit we also eat, drink and wash. The eucharistic communion feeds us, while confession cleanses us. Both should be performed frequently.

In most churches, the sacrament of penance is administered in confessionals, the wooden boxes which stand in the side-aisles. But custom also allows penitents to be received in small rooms, in which a longer dialogue is possible.

1. "The mystery of wickedness is already at work . . . And therefore God sends on them a power that deludes people so that they believe what is false, and so that those who do not believe the truth and take their pleasure in wickedness may all be condemned." (2 Thes 2:7, 11-12)
2. Mt 9:1-8
3. "Receive the Holy Spirit. If you forgive anyone's sins, they are forgiven; if you retain anyone's sins, they are retained." (Jn 20:22-23)

Confessionals in the basilica of Saint Sabina on the Aventine in Rome.

ANOINTING OF THE SICK

FOR THE SICK, ANOINTMENT
ALLEVIATES SUFFERING BY BRINGING
PEACE TO THEIR SOULS

THE GOSPELS REPORT THAT CHRIST CURED THE SICK AND BROUGHT THEM TO THEIR FEET BY THE LAYING-ON OF HANDS.[1] HE EVEN introduced the apostles to this form of contact, adding to it anointment with oil.[2] This is an expression of humanity and divine tenderness. Above and beyond this symbolic gesture, which constitutes the sacrament of Anointing the Sick, God and the Church support and gently care for those with bodily suffering, as well as for the old and dying. This tangible sign of solicitude is the last of the seven sacraments, which accompany us throughout our lives.

From the earliest apostolic times (first century), the practice of the laying-on of hands on the sick became widespread. "Any one of you who is ill" wrote Saint James in his Epistle, "should send for the elders (*presbuteroi* in Greek, hence "priests") of the church, and they must anoint the sick person with oil in the name of the Lord and pray over him. The prayer of faith will save the sick person and the Lord will raise him up again; and if he has committed any sins, he will be forgiven" (Jer 5:14-15). It is thus a sign of physical as well as spiritual healing, which is concluded by absolution. The administration of the sacrament by a priest involves the silent laying-on of hands, and anointment with the oil for

anointing the sick (blessed by the bishop on Maundy Thursday during the chrism mass) on the forehead and the hands, accompanied by these words: "[Name], through this holy anointing, may the Lord in his love and mercy help you with the grace of the Holy Spirit. May the Lord who frees you from sin save you and raise you up."

The expression "Extreme Unction" is better known than the "Anointing of the Sick", although the latter is more exact. Extreme Unction was given only when death was imminent, when the sick were *in extremis*. In a superstitious way, the family waited for the last possible moment before calling in the priest with his oils and viaticum (the last communion), for his visit was generally considered to be a sign of death. The Second Vatican Council reintroduced a custom of anointing the sick which is more consistent with its beginnings.

It is, therefore, not necessary to wait until the last moment before asking for anointment; a serious illness, any major operation, or simply the onset of old age, are reason enough to receive it in faith, with the alleviation of the body and soul which it always brings.

1. Mk 6:5; Mt 8:3-15
2. Mk 6:13

Sacramental anointment of a believer's palm with oil.

64

SONG
AND MUSIC

AS HIGHER EXPRESSIONS OF HUMAN FEELING,
SONG AND MUSIC UNITE OUR HEARTS IN PRAYER

PERSONAL PRAYER IS MADE IN SILENT CON-CENTRATION, FROM A SIMPLE ATTACHMENT OF LOVE. THE LITURGY WHICH UNITES a community is a symphony which presupposes that its various instruments are tuned together. As the Old Testament puts it: "Praise him with fanfare of trumpet, praise him with harp and lyre, praise him with tambourines and dancing, praise him with strings and pipes, praise him with the clamour of cymbals, praise him with triumphant cymbals. Let everything that breathes praise Yahweh. Alleluia!" (Ps 150:3-6). As in many religions, which make song into a higher register of human expression, the voice is the most beautiful instrument of divine praise, and the organ, which is a sort of orchestra all on its own, is its best accompaniment for sacred music. "Whoever loves singing," said Saint Augustine, "and who sings well, prays twice over."

Derived from the Greek word *psalmos*, "the plucking of a string," a psalm is a poem sung to God, accompanied by a cithara or a lute. For both Jews and Christians, the Book of Psalms is the perfect expression of personal and communal prayer. There are 150 psalms, attributed to King David, which express to God the full range of human feelings when "touched" by misfortune or happiness, persecution, fear or tenderness. In turn, we fill them with our experiences and expectations when we sing them in a choir. They are a sort of love-song from the Bride, who tells the Bridegroom of her joy, and her sufferings.

Different centuries and cultures have left us with many forms of religious song and music, among which Gregorian Plainsong remains "specially suited to the Roman liturgy."[1] Attributed to Pope Gregory I, who more than anything established the texts, this repertoire adapts and extends the psalms with the strength and the beauty of a profound interior knowledge. Its origins are extremely ancient, and it flourished between the Loire and the Rhine in the eighth and ninth centuries. After that, it spread across the whole of the Christian West, where it is still sung by numerous monastic communities.

In order to unite the faithful in a single prayer, there are also many other songs, whose force depends on their biblical inspiration, and which are sung in our various mother tongues— for example the chorales in German and English. Even today, music and song, when linked with different cultures, are a part of any religious celebration. They are a beautiful homage to God, which also honour those who sing them.

1. Constitution of the Sacred Liturgy of the Second Vatican Council, N°116

In the basilica of Montmartre, the Benedictines of the Sacré-Cœur sing the praises of God.

GESTURES
AND POSTURES

WHETHER ALONE OR GATHERED TOGETHER, PEOPLE
SPEAK TO GOD THROUGH THE MOVEMENT OF THEIR BODIES

RATHER THAN A CONCERTO, IN WHICH A
SOLO INSTRUMENT IS SET OFF AGAINST THE
ORCHESTRA, THE CATHOLIC LITURGY IS A
symphony: each instrument is an essential element of the overall work, playing its own part and
playing it to the full. But this musical metaphor is
not quite good enough, for, apart from the voices
and instruments, the liturgical act also demands
the participation of the whole of man: his soul,
his spirit, his heart, and his body. A better image
would be that of an opera, which also figures the
actors' movements and postures. This is no easy
comparison, for the notion of *Opus Dei*, which
has been spread by the rule of Saint Benedict,
means "the Work of God", that is to say both the
work he consecrates to us and that which he
accomplishes through us and for us; it should not
be forgotten that the word "opera" comes from
the Latin *opera*, "works", the plural of *opus*.

Even though Christian liturgy cannot be
said to be choreographed, it nevertheless implies
precise organization of the movements of its various participants. Its ceremonial side is a necessity, so that the liturgical rites can take place in
absolute peace and communicate a sensation of
sacredness to the faithful, that is to say God's
active and loving presence.

According to the context, liturgical celebrations
ask us to adopt four different stable positions of
the entire body: standing, sitting, kneeling and,
more rarely, prostration.

The standing position is the most noble
because it characterizes mankind, created in
God's image. It is also a sign of the respect which
man bears the sacred and which is appropriate,
for example, to the reading of the Gospels. We
stand upright before God when praying, generally
turned towards the East, that is to say towards the
rising sun, the symbol of the resurrected Christ.
That is why the choir in churches is generally
"orientated" towards the East. The sitting position represents peaceful openness, more fitted for
listening to readings or sermons. We kneel down
to show a more intense supplication, or for hum-
bler and more intimate prayers, in the mass during the consecration, and also for the adoration of
the Holy Sacrament.

Prostration consists in lying stretched out
on the ground. It is reserved for solemn moments.
Thus, during the singing of the litany of the
saints, the ordinand is prostrated before receiving
the sacrament of Holy Orders, as is the person
who is about to pronounce his religious vows. On
Good Friday, after the reading of the Passion

*Preceding pages: left, Roman antiphonary, Lyons, 1716; right, the lesser
Cavaillé-Coll organ (in Saint Anne's, Kergonan).
Opposite: hands put together symbolize the intensity of prayer.*

70

according to Saint John which tells of the death of Jesus, the lector stops for a moment and the whole congregation prostrates itself.

The hands and the arms of the celebrant play a very important part in the carrying-out of a liturgical rite, in blessings, anointments, and particularly in consecrations. As a symbol of the purity he requires, the priest washes his fingers after the offertory and after the communion. Hands are put together in a gesture of supplication and they are kept together when a priest is officiating during a ceremony and when he has nothing to do or to hold. Sometimes the celebrant stretches his hands and arms out, for example during the recitation of the Lord's Prayer in the mass. This is the ancient posture of the Orant, which has been found depicted in the catacombs from the earliest Christian times. The hands are the best instruments for the administration of the sacraments, and the bishop lays them on the candidate during ordination.

The liturgy also requires the faithful to make several gestures with their hands: they cross their foreheads, stomachs and shoulders. At the moment of the announcement of the Gospel, the thumb traces a small sign of the cross over the forehead, mouth and heart. When the faithful shake hands, which commonly replaces the kiss of peace which is mutually given before the communion, this is a sign of the chaste affection which they have for one another.

There are also other rites which involve other parts of the body. The mass on the evening of Maundy Thursday includes the washing of feet which reenacts Christ's gesture during the Last Supper.[1] The faithful bow their heads before the symbols of the divine presence: the altar, the cross, and the book of the Gospels. Monks bow down low at the end of each psalm when they chant the "Glory be to the Father and to the Son and to the Holy Spirit" during the celebration of their offices. A genuflexion is a requirement in all churches when passing in front of the Holy Sacrament, whose presence is indicated on the altar by an ever-burning light.

During a funeral, the body of the deceased is sprinkled with holy water as a sign of purification and thurified as a sign of respect because, according to Saint Paul, our bodies are the members of Christ and temples of the Holy Spirit.[2] They are called upon to enter, transfigured, into the heavenly liturgy.

During certain ceremonies, the entire congregation walks towards the Lord, just as the Bride goes to join her Groom. The best-known examples of these processions take place on February 2, after the blessing of the candles, on Palm Sunday, or at the moment of entering the church at the beginning of the Easter Vigil, after the blessing of the Paschal Candle. On Corpus Christi Day, the processions of the Holy Sacrament are even more important. The frequency of such processions varies according to the country or region. There are, for example, more of them in Lourdes, where processions with torches are extremely popular.

1. "No one who has had a bath needs washing, such a person is clean all over. You too are clean . . ." (Jn 13:10)
2. 1 Cor 6:15-19

Arms stretched out in the ancient gesture of prayer; they also symbolize the availability of the priest, and are a sign of God's presence.

SACRED VESTMENTS

WHEN OFFICIATING IN THE NAME OF GOD, CELEBRANTS WEAR CERTAIN SPECIFIC ORNAMENTS

EARLIER IN THE BOOK, A PARALLEL WAS DRAWN BETWEEN CATHOLIC LITURGY AND AN OPERA. SUCH A COMPARISON MAY BE extended to the use of costumes, as celebrants are obliged to wear particular vestments when carrying out sacred rites.

The Book of Revelation often talks of the heavenly liturgy, with its instruments, songs, processions and assorted movements. Saint John saw: "a huge number . . . standing in front of the throne and in front of the Lamb, dressed in white robes and holding palms in their hands. They shouted in a loud voice, 'Salvation to our God, who sits on the throne, and to the Lamb!'"(Rv 7:9-10).

The white robes of the chosen, a symbol of the purity they need in order to meet God, is also reminiscent of the dress of the angels who announce the Resurrection of Christ to the holy women. Equally, the newly baptized receive a white robe, which is the sign of their inner rebirth. During the solemn communion, the communicants wear white albs, which is also the primary vestment of all ministers during liturgical rites, whatever their function; a variant of these robes are worn by those who have received the sacrament of Holy Orders.

- Alb (from the Latin *alba*, "white"): the alb is a white robe with long sleeves which covers the entire body, and which is gathered at the waist by a cord. When the alb has neither a hood nor a collar, an amice is worn around the neck. The alb is the basic vestment of all those who take part in liturgical ceremonies: bishops, priests, deacons, acolytes (servers) and lectors. Some servers also wear white surplices over red or black soutanes.

- Stole (from the Latin *stola*, "long robe", which became a liturgical vestment during the eighth century): worn above the alb, it is the minimum that ordained ministers can wear as vestments. It consists of a long strip of cloth made up of two equal bands. Bishops and priests wear it round the neck and the two bands hang down in front parallel to each other. Deacons wear it across their chests, coming down from the left shoulder. A stitch or a small knot at the bottom joins the two parts together, so that the stole forms a diagonal all round the body, in front as well as behind, like a bandoleer.

- Chasuble (from the Latin *casula*, "small house"): the chasuble is a capacious upper vestment, put over the head like a poncho. It completely envelops the wearer and protects him like a small house, or a tent. It is the vestment which

the bishop or priest wears when celebrating the mass; in the chasuble they "put on" the presence of Christ to act in his place during the eucharistic sacrifice. The capaciousness of the early chasuble, has been reintroduced, but we can still find "violin-case" chasubles of the baroque period, so called because they are rectangular at the back, while at the front they are shaped like a violin case, allowing the priest free use of his arms. Chasubles are generally ornate, and are sometimes even richly embroidered.

- Dalmatic (from Dalmatia, now Croatia): in solemn ceremonies the dalmatic is the vestment worn by deacons (that is to say "servants", symbols of Christ the Servant) over the alb and the stole. As far as Christians are concerned, "to serve is to reign." This capacious tunic which is split under the arms, ornate like the chasuble and with short sleeves, was originally part of the dress of Roman emperors and of certain Popes in the High Middle Ages.

- Cape (from the Latin *cappa*, "hooded cloak"): a long ceremonial cloak covering the entire body, the cape consists of a semi-circular piece of cloth, with its two folds held together at the front by hooks and eyes. The cape is worn during solemn offices outside the mass. The celebrant wears it over his alb and stole, and it can also be worn by assistants and cantors.

- Liturgical colours: liturgical vestments (and ornaments) are coloured according to a set of rules. White signifies the time of Christmas and Easter, as well as festivals of saints who were not martyrs. Violet is worn during Advent and Lent, which are times of preparation or penance.

Pink is for the third Sunday of Advent and the fourth Sunday of Lent. Red is for Good Friday, Pentecost and the festivals of martyrs. Green is for ordinary periods. In certain regions, gold is worn for solemn rites, blue for the Virgin Mary and black for the deceased.

These highly symbolic vestments are set aside for the celebrant and those who surround him, because they are the representatives or servants of Christ. This should not create the impression that a celebration of the liturgy is a show put on in front of an audience of the faithful; there is only one congregation in which each person fulfils his role and participates in the celebration of the mystery of the Eucharist, in perfect harmony with and as complements to all the others. The faithful, too, can put on the clothes of Christ, as is witnessed by the white vestment which they receive during baptism and religious profession.

At the tailor Gammarelli's in Rome, embroidered orphreys and galloons destined for liturgical vestments.

78

PONTIFICAL INSIGNIA

THE MITRE AND THE CROOK, THE PASTORAL HEADDRESS AND STAFF, MAKE UP THE BISHOPS' INSIGNIA

A PONTIFF IS SOMEONE WHO ACTS AS A "BRIDGE" BETWEEN TWO PEOPLE (FROM THE LATIN *PONS*). JESUS CHRIST IS THE FINEST example of a pontiff: at once God and man, he unites God to man in the New Covenant. By virtue of their ordination, bishops, the successors to the apostles, exercise this mediating power in the name of Christ, the High Priest. In their midst, the Pope, as the successor of Saint Peter, and as a result the Vicar of Christ, is called the "Sovereign Pontiff".

The insignia which the Pope and the bishops generally wear are the pectoral cross and the ring. During solemn offices, they make use of pontifical insignia, the mitre and the crook, which they received at their ordination into the episcopate.

The mitre is a "headdress". The original Greek *mitra* was a headband, or a diadem. In the Old Testament, the High Priest and the priests wore a turban, decorated with a golden flower, a sign of consecration.[1] The Christian mitre, originally a headband with a veil, has changed during the ages, but was from early times reserved for bishops. It is triangular in form and points upwards. Early mitres were lower. During the baroque period they were heightened and have now returned to more or less reasonable proportions.

The crook, or pastoral staff, is the most typical sign of those who represent, for their church or for their community, the presence of the Good Shepherd. The word comes from "crochet" because of the hook at its tip. In early times, the shepherd's crook was bent at the top into a hook, with a sort of groove which allowed shepherds to throw earth or stones at sheep which had strayed, as well as at predators which came near them. Since Paul VI, the Pope has carried a crook which is topped with a curved cross, which symbolizes his mission to bring together God's scattered sheep.[2] The crook and the mitre are reserved for bishops, but they are also given to father abbots (heads of monastic abbeys) during their abbatial benediction, for they take the place of Christ in their communities.

The pallium, a legacy from the dress of certain Roman dignitaries, is the badge of the Pope and of the archbishops. It is a strip of white wool which is worn round the neck, over the chasuble, like a collar. Two flaps hang down from this broad collar, one in front, the other behind. Six black crosses are embroidered at intervals on the strip of wool.

1. Ex 39:28, 30-31; Lv 8:9   2. Jn 11:52.

Pope John Paul II at the main altar of the basilica of Saint Peter in Rome.
He is wearing his mitre and pallium. Also visible is his crook,
topped off by a slightly curved crucifix.

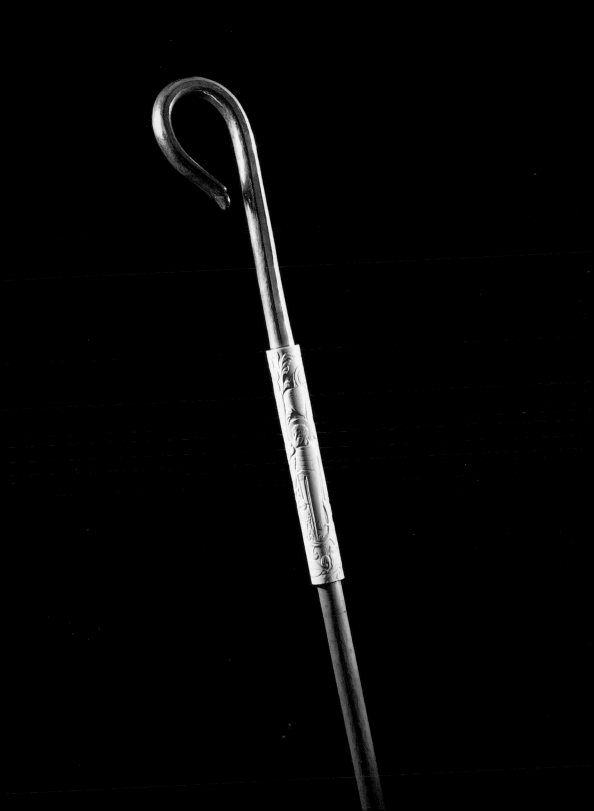

SCRIPTURE

AT THE HEART OF THE PEOPLE OF GOD,
HOLY SCRIPTURE IS THE SUBSTANCE
OF LITURGICAL TEXTS

HOLY SCRIPTURE IS MADE UP OF THE OLD TESTAMENT (COMMON TO BOTH JEWS AND CHRISTIANS) AND THE NEW TESTAMENT, which includes the four Gospels, the Acts of the Apostles, Epistles written by apostles and the Revelation of Saint John. This priceless gem, a superbly detailed history of the People of God culminating with the mystery of Christ, is venerated by all Christians. Yet, while the Protestants consider that reading the Bible is enough to nourish their faith in salvation, the Catholics gain access to Scripture only by means of the Tradition which created it and which has carried it down the ages, according to the Church's living teaching and especially thanks to the liturgy.

There are, then, numerous editions of the Bible, which vary according to different confessions. Catholic editions always include notes of explanation, inspired by the living Tradition of the Church. During the last two decades, some marvellous ecumenical translations have been made, with notes which point out, when necessary, the different churches' interpretations; this is an important step towards Christian unity.

Roman Catholic liturgy is extremely biblical, perhaps even more so than the liturgy of the eastern churches, whose large number of long prayers are still inspired by the Scriptures. We have already seen how the Book of Psalms is the great inspiration behind the celebration of the "Hours". The liturgy of the Word, the first part of the mass and of other offices, consists of readings taken from the Bible, and the most important among them is always a passage from the Gospels.

These readings, which are essential for a true understanding of the liturgy, must be done with skill and respect; the lector is an officially appointed minister. The proclamation of the Gospel is reserved for the celebrant, or for the assisting deacon, and is accompanied by various rites.

The evangelistary is a book worthy of its role, beautifully but soberly bound and decorated. It is laid on the altar at the beginning of the mass, then carried in procession to the ambo (from the Greek *anabaino*, "to go up"), the place of the Word. The cathedra, positioned near the middle of the nave, used to perform this function.

Nowadays, the ambo is placed in the sanctuary, not far from the altar, so that both parts of the mass work together in the best possible way. It consists of a slightly raised platform, equipped with a lectern, from which the lectors and the cantor, the deacons and the celebrant address the congregation. The oldest churches in Rome have preserved magnificent ambos, such as Saint Clement's, which dates to the twelfth century.

Preceding double page: the mitre and crook.
Opposite: an English evangelistary of the eighth century
(Vatican Library, Barb. lat. 570): Saint John the Evangelist.

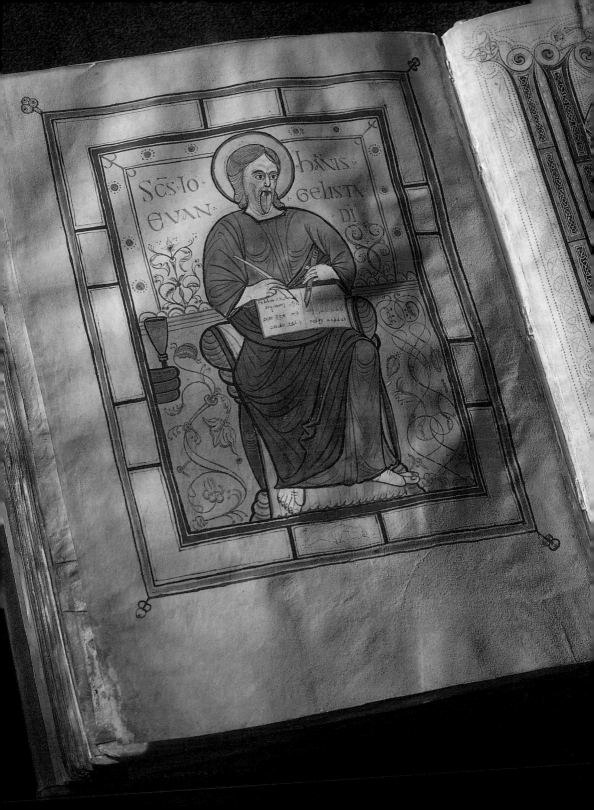

ויאמר אל תקרב הלם של נעליך מעל רגליך כי
המקום אשר אתה עומד עליו אדמת קדש הוא׃
ויאמר אנכי אלהי אביך אלהי אברהם אלהי יצחק
ואלהי יעקב ויסתר משה פניו כי ירא מהביט אל
האלהים׃ ויאמר יהוה ראה ראיתי את עני עמי
אשר במצרים ואת צעקתם שמעתי מפני נגשיו כי
ידעתי את מכאביו׃ וארד להצילו מיד מצרים
ולהעלתו מן הארץ ההוא אל ארץ טובה ורחבה אל
ארץ זבת חלב ודבש אל מקום הכנעני והחתי והאמרי
והפרזי והחוי והיבוסי׃ ועתה הנה צעקת בני
ישראל באה אלי וגם ראיתי את הלחץ אשר מצרים
לחצים אתם׃ ועתה לכה ואשלחך אל פרעה
והוצא את עמי בני ישראל ממצרים׃ ויאמר משה
אל האלהים מי אנכי כי אלך אל פרעה וכי אוציא
את בני ישראל ממצרים׃ ויאמר כי אהיה
עמך וזה לך האות כי אנכי שלחתיך בהוציאך
את העם ממצרים תעבדון את האלהים על
ההר הזה׃ ויאמר משה אל האלהים הנה
אנכי בא אל בני ישראל ואמרתי להם אלהי
אבותיכם שלחני אליכם ואמרו לי מה שמו
מה אמר אלהם׃ ויאמר אלהים אל משה אהיה
אשר אהיה ויאמר כה תאמר לבני ישראל אהיה
שלחני אליכם׃ ויאמר עוד אלהים אל משה
כה תאמר אל בני ישראל יהוה אלהי אבתיכם
אלהי אברהם אלהי יצחק ואלהי יעקב שלחני
אליכם זה שמי לעלם וזה זכרי לדר דר׃ לך
ואספת את זקני ישראל ואמרת אלהם יהוה אלהי
אבתיכם נראה אלי אלהי אברהם יצחק ויעקב
לאמר פקד פקדתי אתכם ואת העשוי לכם
במצרים׃

5 At ille: Non appropies, inquit, huc. Solue calciamentum de pedibus tuis. locus enim in quo stas, terra sancta est. 6 Et ait: Ego sum Deus patris tui, Deus Abraam, Deus Isaac, & Deus Iacob. Abscondit Moyses faciem suam: non enim audebat aspicere contra Deum. 7 Cui ait Dominus: Vidi afflictionem populi mei in Ægypto: & clamorem eius audiui propter duritiam eorum qui præsunt operibus: & sciens dolorem eius: 8 Descendi, vt liberem eum de manibus Ægyptiorum, & educam de terra illa, in terram bonam & spatiosam, in terram quæ fluit lacte & melle, ad loca Chananæi, & Ethæi, & Amorræi, & Pherezæi, & Euæi, & Iebusæi. 9 Clamor ergo filiorum Israel venit ad me, vidique afflictionem eorum, qua ab Ægyptiis opprimuntur. 10 Sed veni, & mittam te ad Pharaonem, vt educas populum meum filios Israel de Ægypto.

11 Dixitque Moyses ad Deum: Quis sum ego, vt vadam ad Pharaonem, & educam filios Israel de Ægypto? 12 Qui dixit ei: Ego ero tecum, & hoc habebis signum, quod miserim te. Cum eduxeris populum de Ægypto, immolabis Deo super montem istum.

13 Ait Moyses ad Deum: Ecce ego vadam ad filios Israel, & dicam eis: Deus patrum vestrorum misit me ad vos. Si dixerint mihi, C Quod est nomen eius, quid dicam eis?

14 Dixit Deus ad Moysen: Ego sum qui sum. Ait: Sic dices filiis Israel: Qui est, misit me ad vos.

15 Dixitque iterum Deus ad Moysen: Hæc dices filiis Israel: Dominus Deus patrum vestrorum Deus Abraam, & Deus Isaac, & Deus Iacob, misit me ad vos. Hoc nomen mihi est in æternum, & hoc memoriale meum in generatione & generationem.

16 Vade, Congrega seniores Israel, & dices ad eos: Dominus Deus patrum vestrorum apparuit mihi, Deus Abraam, & Deus Isaac, & Deus Iacob, dicens: Visitans visitaui vos, & vidi omnia quæ acciderunt vobis in Ægypto.

תרגום אונקלוס

ואמר לא תקרב הלכא שרי סינך מעל רגלך ארי אתרא דאת קאים עלוהי אתר קדיש הוא׃ ואמר אנא אלהיה דאבוך אלהיה דאברהם אלהיה דיצחק ואלהיה דיעקב וכסי משה אפוהי ארי הוה דחיל מלאסתכלא לצית יקרא דיי׃ ואמר יי מגלא גלי קדמי שעבוד עמי די במצרים וית קבילתהון שמיע קדמי מן קדם מפלחיהון ארי גלי קדמי כיביהון׃ ואתגליתי לשזבותהון מידא דמצראי ולאסקותהון מן ארעא ההיא לארע טבא ופתיא לארע עבדא חלב ודבש לאתר כנענאי וחתאי ואמוראי ופריזאי וחואי ויבוסאי׃ וכען הא קבילת בני ישראל עלת לקדמי ואף גלי קדמי דוחקא דמצראי דחקין להון׃ וכען איתא ואשלחנך לות פרעה ואפיק ית עמי בני ישראל ממצרים׃ ואמר משה קדם יי מן אנא ארי איזיל לות פרעה וארי אפיק ית בני ישראל ממצרים׃ ואמר ארי יהי מימרי בסעדך ודין לך אתא ארי אנא שלחתך באפקותך ית עמא ממצרים תפלחון קדם יי על טורא הדין׃ ואמר משה קדם יי הא אנא אתי לות בני ישראל ואימר להון אלהא דאבהתכון שלחני לותכון ויימרון לי מה שמיה מה אימר להון׃ ואמר יי למשה אהיה אשר אהיה ואמר כדנן תימר לבני ישראל אהיה שלחני לותכון׃ ואמר עוד יי למשה כדנן תימר לבני ישראל יי אלהא דאבהתכון אלהיה דאברהם אלהיה דיצחק ואלהיה דיעקב שלחני לותכון דין הוא שמי לעלם ודין דוכרני לכל דר ודר׃ איזיל ותכנוש ית סבי ישראל ותימר להון יי אלהא דאבהתכון אתגלי לי אלהיה דאברהם יצחק ויעקב למימר מדכר דכירנא יתכון וית דאתעביד לכון במצרים׃

[Left column — Latin]

...& ait: Non appropinques huc: solue
...onem de pedibus tuis: & enim locus in quo
...ras, terra sancta est.
...dixit: Ego sum Deus patris tui, Deus A-
...& Deus Isaac, & Deus Iacob. Auertit au-
Moyses faciem suam: timuit enim aspicere con-
...

Dixit autem Dominus ad
...Videns vidi afflictionem populi mei qui
...gypto: & clamorem eorum audiui, propter o-
...præsellas: scio enim dolorem eorum:
Et descendi, vt liberarem eos ex manu Aegyp-
...educam eos ex terra illa, & inducam
...terram bonam & multam,in terram manan-
...& ut locum Chananæorum, & Æthe-
...Amorræorum, & Pherezæorum, & E-
...& Gergesæorum, & Iebusæorum.
Et nunc ecce clamor filiorum Israel venit ad
...& ego vidi afflictionem, qua Ægyptii oppri-
...eos.

Et nunc veni, Mittam te ad Pharaonem re-
Ægypti: & educes populum meum filios Israel
...ex Ægypto.
Et dixit Moyses ad Deum: Quis sum ego, vt
...ad Pharaonem regem Ægypti, & vt edu-
...Israel ex terra Ægypti?
Dixit autem Deus ad Moysen, dicens: Quia
...& hoc tibi signum, quod ego te mitto:
...cum eduxeris populum meum ex Ægypto, & ser-
...Deo in monte hoc.

Et dixit Moyses ad
...Ecce ego vadam ad filios Israel, et dicam ad
...patrum vestrorum misit me ad vos. & si
...quaerint me, Quod nomen est quid dicam ad
...

Et dixit Dominus ad Moysen: Ego sum
...& dixit: Sic dices filiis Israel: Qui est,
...ad vos.

Et dixit Deus rursus ad
...Sic dices filiis Israel: Dominus Deus pa-
...vestrorum, Deus Abraam, & Deus Isaac,
...Iacob, misit me ad vos. hoc meum est no-
...æternum, & memoriale generationum ge-
...bus.

Vadens igitur, congrega seniores
...Israel, & dices ad eos: Dominus Deus pa-
...strorum apparuit mihi, Deus Abraam,
...Isaac, et Deus Iacob, dicens: Visitatione vistram
...quecunq; contigerint vobis in Ægypto, vidi.

[Center and right columns — Greek, largely illegible]

CHALDAICAE PARAPHRASIS TRANSLATIO.

...dixit ei: Non appropinques huc: solue calciamentum tuum de pedibus tuis, quoniam locus super quem in stas, terra sancta est.
...Ego sum Deus patris tui, Deus Abraham, Deus Isaac, & Deus Iacob. Et inclinauit Moyses vultum suum, quoniam timuit aspicere coram Deo.
...Et dixit Dominus: Reuelata est coram me subiectio populi mei qui est in Ægypto: & clamor eorum audiui coram exactoribus eorum.
...conspectu meo, propter exactores eorum, quoniam reuelatus sum dolores eorum.
...Et apparui vt liberarem
...Ethæi, & Amorrei, & Pherezæi, & Euæi, & Iebusæi.
...& vt ascendere faciam eos de terra hac, ad terram bonam & spaciosam, ad terram fluentem lacte & melle, ad locum Cha-
...me in tribulatio qua Ægyptii tribulant eos.
...Et nunc ecce clamor filiorum Israel venit coram me: manifesta est
...de Ægypto.
...Et dixit: Quia est verbum meum in adiutorium tuum. & vt educam filios Israel de Æ-
...Ægypto, seruietis coram Domino super montem hunc.
...Et dixit Moyses coram Deo: Ecce ego vadam ad fi-
...& dicam eis: Deus patrum vestrorum misit me ad vos. & dicent mihi: Quod est nomen eius? quid dicam eis?
...dixit Deus ad Moysen: Ero qui ero. & dixit: Sic dices filiis Israel, Qui ero, misit me ad vos.
...Dixitque iterum
Moysi: Hæc dices filiis Israel. Dominus Deus patrum vestrorum, Deus Abraham, Deus Isaac, & Deus Iacob misit me ad vos. hoc est no-
...meum æternum, & hoc est memoriale meum in omni generatione & generationem.
...Vade, & congrega seniores Israel,
...Dominus Deus patrum vestrorum apparuit mihi, Deus Abraham, Isaac, & Iacob, dicens: Recordans recordatus sum vestri, & quic...
...sunt vobis in Ægypto.

THE ALTAR

AT THE CENTRE OF THE CHURCH,
THE ALTAR IS BOTH THE PLACE OF SACRIFICE
AND THE COMMUNION TABLE

THE ALTAR IS THE MEETING POINT BETWEEN GOD AND MANKIND, THE TRUE CENTRE OF ALL RELIGIOUS BUILDINGS, POSITIONED AT THE heart of the sanctuary, raised up on a few steps so that the architecture is drawn towards it. The word "altar" is derived from the Latin adjective *altus*, meaning "high". Mankind has always led him to put his places of worship on high; Mount Olympus was the dwelling-place of the Greek gods. When no natural heights are available, the sanctuary is placed on the top of an artificial structure, as can be seen in the ziggurats of Mesopotamia. When man wanted to force his way into the holy kingdom, he thought up the Tower of Babel. Jewish tradition considers that mountains are the natural places to meet God, there, where heaven and earth touch. It was at the summit of Mount Sinai that Yahweh spoke to Moses.

As a sign of respect for divine transcendance, the smoke of offerings was first made to "go up" towards God who "smelt the pleasing smell" (Gn 8:21). This is the tradition of sacrifice by fire, the holocaust (from the Greek *holokaustos*, "entirely burnt"). In the rite inspired by the Covenant on Mount Sinai, Moses shared the blood of the victims between the altar he had just built, which represents God, and the people whom he sprinkled with it. Yahweh and Israel thus became "of one blood."[1] The New Christian Covenant continues this "consanguinity" and makes us into God's table guests, since the sacrifice of the communion feeds the congregation with the very body and blood of Christ himself. The altars in our churches are tables where these offerings are laid out. They are symbols of God, who receives the gifts which are offered by the congregation of the faithful. But the altar is also a communal table at which the guests share the sacred meal. Christ is, at once the altar, as God who receives the sacrifice, the priest, and the victim, as the man who offers it and who offers himself.

During the dedication of churches, the first thing is to seal up relics of saints—or, originally, of martyrs—inside the altar in order to mark the continuity between Christ's sacrifice and that of his faithful. The altar is then consecrated with an anointment of holy chrism. After that, it is illuminated by the burning of incense, which is the sign of the Holy Spirit's taking possession of it. Finally, it is laid with altar cloths.

The altar is, then, the most elevated symbol of Christ in the church. Even before the cross, it is the first object which we venerate when entering. The priest kisses it at the beginning and the end of the mass as a sign of respect.

1. Ex 24:4-8

Preceding double pages: left, the ambo of Saint Clement's in Rome (twelfth century); right and verso, polyglot Bible of Plantin, Antwerp, 1569-1571. Opposite: altar of the chapel of Locadour (Morbihan, France).

BREAD AND WINE

THE BREAD AND THE WINE, TRANSFORMED
RESPECTIVELY INTO THE BODY AND BLOOD OF JESUS,
MAKE THE RISEN CHRIST PRESENT AMONG US

BREAD AND WINE ARE UNIVERSAL SYMBOLS OF WHAT BRINGS US LIFE: FOOD AND DRINK. THE PSALMIST THANKS GOD FOR SATISFYING mankind's needs: "for cattle you make the grass grow, and for people the plants they need, to bring forth food from the earth, and wine to cheer people's hearts" (Ps 104:14-15).

Thus Christ chose the simplest of elements as the sacred signs of his grace. Christians nourish themselves with bread and wine, which have become the body and blood of the Lord Jesus. As far as the Catholic and Orthodox churches are concerned a real transformation of substance occurs during the consecration, the "transubstantiation". This belief is shared by High Church Anglicans and certain Lutherans, but for most Protestants the bread and the wine are nothing more than symbols (in the broadest sense of the term) of Christ and not his actual presence.

The separation of Christ's body and blood is obviously a symbol of his death on the Cross. Their actual presence is witness of the renewal of the sacrifice of the Eucharist, inaugurated by Jesus himself during the Last Supper. This body and this blood must be given as nourishment to the faithful, following Christ's words: "Anyone who does eat my flesh and drink my blood has eternal life, and I shall raise that person up on the last day. For my flesh is real food and my blood is real drink . . . As the living Father sent me and I draw life from the Father, so whoever eats me will also draw life from me" (Jn 6:54-57).

Whoever receives the communion of the Eucharist is truly given the life of Jesus, through the Father, and thus also through the mystery of the Trinity which unites in love the Father, the Son and the Holy Spirit. We are invited to the "holy table" and are received there as guests to share with Jesus his life as the Son at the heart of the Trinity.

The bread of the Eucharist consists of small wafers of unleavened bread, which are called hosts. This word is a link between the Christian communion and sacrifice, for the Latin word *hostia* means a sacrificial victim, and this is the sense in which Saint Paul uses it when talking of Christ.[1] Unleavened bread was the only sort permitted in the Jewish rite of the Passover[2] and that is why it was consecrated by Jesus during the Last Supper. For this reason, the Roman Church does not permit the consecration of ordinary bread, as opposed to the Orthodox churches which celebrate the Eucharist with leavened bread. The disputes which were once caused by these diverging customs have fortunately lost their bitterness during the last few centuries.

Preceding double page: left, the bare sanctuary of the abbey church of Saint Anne,
Kergonan; right, the abundantly decorated choir of a church in Latin America.
Opposite: the large host of the celebrant and the small hosts of the faithful.

In the West, a distinction is made between the small hosts for the faithful (which are easy to distribute and to receive) and the large ones for the priests (so that they are easily visible when raised after consecration). Nowadays thicker ones are produced and their baking sometimes gives them a colour which is more golden than white.

At the beginning of the mass, the hosts which are to be consecrated are placed in one or more patens (from the Latin *patena*, "a shallow dish"), which are convex, circular, and made of precious metals plated with gold or silver. They can also be made of other fine elements and some patens are masterpieces of the goldsmith's art. The same is true for the ciborium (from the Greek *kiborion*, "the fruit of the water-lily" and, by extension, a cup shaped like this fruit) in which the hosts are placed for the assembled faithful. The ciborium is a hemispherical cup, closed with a cover, which is often topped by a cross. Outside the mass, it is kept in the tabernacle to hold "the Reserved Sacrament", which are the consecrated hosts which have not been distributed during the communion. It is then covered by a "canopy", a piece of cloth in the shape of a round tent.

During the adoration of the Holy Sacrament, the consecrated host is presented to the faithful in a monstrance (from the Latin *monstrare*, "to show"). It consists of a piece of gold or silver plate, decorated with an ornamental motif, centred on a circular base (the "lunette" or "little moon", decked with two glass discs) on which the host is placed. The monstrance very often creates the effect of a gleaming sun around the Holy Sacrament.

When the Holy Sacrament is not being dis-played it is kept in the tabernacle in a metal box called a custodial (from the Latin *custodire*, "to keep") or a pyx (from the Greek *pyxis*, "a box"). The pyx is also the name of those small circular boxes which are used for taking the communion to the sick.

The *Code of Canon Law* gives a precise description of communion wine: "The wine must be natural, made from grapes of the vine, and not corrupt" (canon 924). It must therefore be the result of the fermentation of pure grape juice. During the Last Supper, it was the "fruit of the vine" which Jesus transformed into his own blood at the end of the meal. The traditional Passover meal includes four cups of wine and it was the fourth one, the cup of *Hallel* (the adulatory praise of Psalms 114-117), which Christ consecrated.[3]

Since the time of the Old Testament wine has been one of the fundamental symbols of the messianic feast at which, according to Isaiah, must be served "well-strained wines" (Is 25:6). The eucharistic sacrifice and communion make the Last Supper and Calvary a present reality for us, by giving the faithful a foretaste of the feast of the Kingdom to come.

For the consecration of the wine during the mass, the Roman Church generally uses white wine, which will not stain any vestments with which it may come into contact. The celebrant pours it into a chalice (from the Greek *kylix*, in Latin *calix*, "drinking-cup"), which is generally a fine piece of goldsmithery. The style of chalices has changed during the ages. They are often decorated with eucharistic symbols or phrases from the Scriptures.

A plain chalice.

The way in which they are produced means that the bread and the wine are also symbols of the unity of the believers who partake of them. This is explained in one of the most ancient Christian texts, the *Didache*, or "Teaching of the Lord to the Gentiles," which dates to the end of the first century A.D.: "Even as this bread which we break was once scattered through the hills and has been gathered and moulded into one, may thy Church be gathered together from the ends of the earth in thy Kingdom! For thine is the glory and the power for ever and ever." The same can be said for the multitude of grapes: pressed together, they become one single wine. Thus, the faithful who break the bread and drink the cup of salvation, who, in other words, eat the body of Christ and drink his blood, grow up into adult members of the Mystical Body of Christ,[4] which is his Church.

While dealing with the Eucharist, we should mention a custom which would do well to be revived: the *Benedicite* at the beginning of a meal, and grace at its conclusion. This is also a Jewish rite, derived from the numerous blessings or *berakoth* which mark different moments of the day. In family ritual the ancient blessing of meals, the *Birkat-ha-Mazon*, was of central importance. Here is an extract: "Blessed art thou, Lord God, King of the Universe, thou who feedest the whole earth from thy bounty, grace, tenderness and mercy . . . Day after day, thou takest care to do us a multitude of good things. It is thou that multiplieth us for ever in thy grace, tenderness, spirit, mercy and all that is good." During the offertory of the Catholic mass, the two prayers of presentation of the bread and the wine are blessings of this sort. Even more profoundly, the blessing of a meal lies at the root of the Christian Eucharist.

Christians must keep the benefits which God's love gives them permanently in mind, and thank him constantly, even if the path they have been given to follow is beset with a variety of difficulties. These acts of grace (which is, in fact, the original meaning of the word "Eucharist") pass through Jesus Christ, even as, according to Saint Paul, grace comes to us through him: "Blessed be God the Father of our Lord Jesus Christ, who has blessed us with all the spiritual blessings of heaven in Christ" (Ep 1:3).

Through respect for bread and for what it signifies in the Church, for the person into whom it is transformed by the Eucharist, it is a Christian custom not to throw any of it away and, before slicing a loaf, a cross is first traced over it with the knife.

---

1. ". . . and follow Christ by loving as he loved you, giving himself up for us as an offering and a sweet-smelling sacrifice to God (*tradidit semetipsum hostiam deo in odorem suavitatis*)." (Ep 5:2)
2. Ex 12:8
3. Mt 26:29
4. Ep 4:12-16; Col 2:19

At the end of the eucharistic prayer ("Through him, with him, in him")
the priest presents the paten, and the deacon the chalice.

THE TABERNACLE

THE TABERNACLE, WHERE THE
CONSECRATED HOSTS ARE KEPT, IS THE "TENT"
IN WHICH GOD DWELLS AMONG US

THE LATIN *TABERNACULUM* WAS ORIGINALLY A TENT. IN THE HISTORY OF SALVATION, THE PRESENCE OF GOD AMIDST HIS PEOPLE IN exodus was symbolized by the "Tent of Meeting", where Moses went to converse with Yahweh in the name of the People, "as a man talks to his friend" (Ex 33:11). In the New Testament, Saint Paul compares the very humanity of Christ to a tent which was not made by human hands.[1] The Greek text of the prologue to the Gospel according to Saint John contains these very words: "The Word became flesh, he lived [in the Greek *eskenosen*, "pitched his tent"] among us" (Jn 1:14).

The tabernacle in our churches is that small, ornate, locked cupboard on a wall or a side-altar in which the Holy Sacrament is kept. Hosts consecrated during a mass were originally kept for the sick or dying (the viaticum), which is still the case today. During the last few centuries, thanks to an increase in eucharistic devotion, the Reserved Sacrament has also become an object of long, silent adoration.

Two signs show that the tabernacle is inhabited. Firstly it is covered by a canopy (from the Greek *konopion*, "a mosquito net"), a veil of the liturgical colour of the season (violet, white or green). When the tabernacle is cylindrical, this canopy or "grand pavilion" really does make it look like a tent. The other sign of the Lord's actual presence is the lamp which constantly burns beside the tabernacle, the symbolism of which goes back to the Old Testament.[2] Rather than an electric night-light, what should be used is an oil-lamp with a live wick, which is generally placed in a red glass. This is also a symbol of the soul, which is invited to burn itself up before God by consuming its time for him.

But there should be no confusion between signs and symbols. That is why the tabernacle must not be kept on the main altar which is, as we have already explained, an essential symbol of Christ. It must therefore be kept free and clear, with or without its cloths and light. The Lord Jesus, who is actually present in the hosts kept in the tabernacle, must be worshipped, but not on the main altar. For this reason, the tabernacle is fixed on the wall of the sanctuary, or better still on the altar of one of the church's side-chapels, such as the cathedral's axial chapel which opens out on to the middle of the ambulatory.

1. He 9:11.
2. Ex 27:20; 1 Sm 3:3

A tabernacle in the basilica of the Sacré-Cœur in Montmartre. On the door can be seen the Lamb and the seven seals of the Apocalypse (Rv 5:1-9).

CANDLES

AS WARM AND HUMBLE
LIVING FLAMES, CANDLES SYMBOLIZE, ACCOMPANY
AND EXTEND OUR PRAYERS

ORIGINALLY, CANDLES WERE SIMPLY A MEANS OF ILLUMINATION. IN THE CATACOMBS, SMALL OIL-LAMPS WERE USED, WHICH THE Lord alluded to in his parable of the ten virgins,[1] who are symbols of the watchful anticipation of the faithful. Going beyond any practical need for light, Christians have continued to use candles for symbolic purposes. When an altar has just been consecrated by anointment, it is covered with cloths, then candles are arranged around it. Almost all liturgical ceremonies make use of this warming light, which is a familiar part of Catholic celebrations (it is also used by Orthodox Christians, Protestants and Jews).

Light is inextricably linked with Christ, who declared: "I am the light of the world" (Jn 8:12). The *Credo* speaks of him as being "light from light." Christians are "children of light" (Ep 5:8) who no longer want to live in the shadows. When giving a lighted candle at the end of the rite of baptism, the celebrant illustrates this by saying: "Receive the light of Christ."

A blessing of candles, followed by a procession, takes place before the mass on February 2, during the celebration of the Presentation of the Lord at the Temple, which is called Candlemas. In the Gospel reading of that day, old Simeon, in his *Nunc Dimittis*, sees in the child he is holding in his arms "a light of revelation for the gentiles"

(Lk 2:32). The best-known example of a sacred light is the Paschal Candle, a symbol of the risen Christ. The Easter Vigil, the high point of the entire liturgical year, begins by the solemn blessing of the candle. This is an adaptation of the Jewish rite which ordered the lighting of lamps on the Friday evening at the beginning of the Sabbath. It became the lucernarium (from the Latin *lucerna*, "lamp") of the early Church.

The celebrant engraves several symbols of Christ on to the Paschal Candle: the Cross; alpha and omega, which are the first and last letters of the Greek alphabet;[2] finally the four digits of the number of the year. Five grains of incense are then melted into the centre and the four extremities of the cross, as reminders of the five wounds of Christ crucified: in the hands, the feet and in the side. The candle is lit from a freshly kindled light and carried into the church in procession, while the deacon proclaims three times "The Light of Christ." The candle burns only during the fifty days of the Easter period but, in the hearts of the baptized, it must never be allowed to go out. During funeral ceremonies, the Paschal Candle is lighted near the coffin as a sign of hope.

1. Mt 25:1-13
2. "'I am the Alpha and the Omega,' says the Lord God." (Rv 1:8)

In front of a statue or an icon, candles perpetuate the prayers of those who have offered them.

INCENSE

THE PLEASANT SCENT OF INCENSE FILLS THE CHURCH
WITH THE FRAGRANCE OF GOD'S PRESENCE

INCENSE IS AN AROMATIC GUM FROM THE EAST WHICH, WHEN BURNT, GIVES OFF A PERFUMED SMOKE (FROM THE LATIN *incensum*, "something that is burnt"). Aromatic substances, such as benzoin, are often added to incense. It used to be burnt in order to purify houses or tents, like joss-sticks.

Religions make great use of incense, which creates a particular atmosphere, and a sort of welcoming presence in holy places. God himself told Moses to offer it twice a day in front of the sanctuary.[1] The smoke from incense is clearly visible and ascends in soft whirls, which symbolize prayers mounting up to God: "May my prayer be like incense in your presence" (Ps 141:2). At the very threshold of the New Testament, it was while he was making this same offering that Zechariah was told by the Archangel Gabriel about the birth of John the Baptist.[2] This part of the liturgy is closely related to heavenly liturgy: "Another angel, who had a golden censer, came and stood at the altar. A large quantity of incense was given to him to offer with the prayers of all the saints on the golden altar that stood in front of the throne; and so from the angel's hand the smoke of the incense went up in the presence of God and with it the prayers of the saints" (Rv 8:3-4).

Incense is thus a homage of adoration given to God, like the gift, offered by the Wise Men to the infant Jesus: through frankincense, they recognize that he is God, through gold, that he is a King, and myrrh foreshadows his sepulture.[3] Given firstly to God, incense is also received by everything that it touches, and everything that belongs to him: the Cross, the altar, the book of the Gospels, the bread and the wine before and after consecration, but also the celebrants and the faithful, even the deceased. During a funeral, their mortal remains, which were the temple of the Spirit, are thurified.

For the burning of incense, a censer is used. This is a portable fragrance-burner suspended from three chains, with a cover that can be moved by means of a fourth one. Censers with only one chain can also be found. With the help of a spoon, the celebrant takes some incense from an incense-boat and places it on the burning coals contained in the cassolette. The smoke is then spread by swaying the censer. The server in charge of this delicate, complex instrument is called a thurifer, "a carrier of incense" (from the Latin *thus*, "incense" and *ferre*, "to carry"). In Eastern Orthodox churches, incense is very often used in front of icons and is normally highly perfumed (often with roses).

1. Ex 30:7-8
2. Lk 1:9-11
3. Mt 2:11

"From the angel's hand the smoke of the incense went up in the presence of God and with it the prayers of the saints." (Rv 8:4)

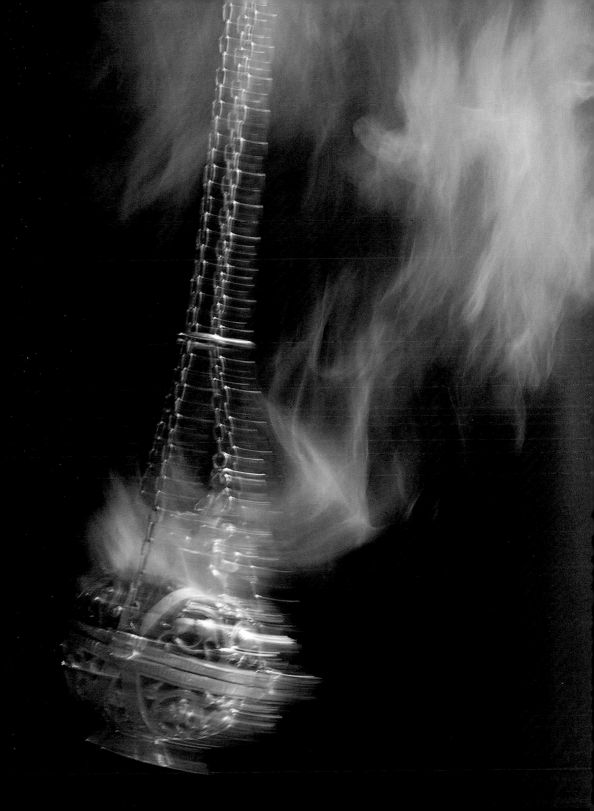

WATER

THE WATER WHICH WASHES AND PURIFIES,
ALSO RESTORES IN THE SOUL THE FRESHNESS OF ITS YOUTH

AS A VITAL AND FAMILIAR ELEMENT IN HUMAN EXISTENCE, WATER HAS ALWAYS BEEN FULL OF SIGNIFICANCE. IN ANCIENT VIEWS OF the world, it was considered to be at the origin of all things and, in order to serve life, it had to be fecundated by the Breath of God.[1] If left to its own devices, water could carry everything away into death and primeval chaos (the flood and the sea). Thus, it is an ambivalent symbol which evokes simultaneously life and death, purification and sanctification.

The various ablutions and sprinklings of water in religious rites, like the blessing and the asperges at the beginning of Sunday mass, or the washing of the hands during the offertory, are first and foremost acts of purification, that is to say that they wash away any faults or stains which would be improper to the celebration of the liturgy.[2] In its positive aspect, water is the basis of life and a symbol of birth and rebirth.[3]

Liturgical rites are effective only if they involve the action of God. Baptism with water—that of John the Baptist—was merely a preparation for the baptism with water and the Spirit which the Son of God instituted.[4] When enlivened by the Spirit, water becomes one of its finest symbols. It received this consecration during the baptism of Jesus in the Jordan, becoming that "living water" which is a "gift of God", that is to say the Spirit itself which, being at the heart of the life of the Trinity, can alone come "welling up for eternal life" (Jn 4:10-14). When plunged into the life and death of Christ through baptism, the sons of God receive the Spirit as a "pledge" which waters and quenches them, while they wait to be immersed in the River of Life which flows from between the throne of God and the Lamb.[5]

The rivers of living water began to flow at the moment of Christ's death on the Cross, at the very hour when Jesus "gave up his spirit" (Jn 19:30) and let the blood and water spring out of his pierced heart as symbols of the sacraments which would henceforth operate through the force of the Spirit.

The blessing of water, to which holy salts can be added (a symbol of preservation and flavour), is a church tradition. The sprinkling of holy water is performed during many rites of blessing. It is sprinkled on the mortal remains of Christians, on their coffins, and on their tombs. At the entrance to churches, the basin of holy water is an invitation to the faithful to cross themselves after wetting the tips of their fingers in it. Holy water can also be requested and taken home. This is an act of faith, linked to the mystery of the Cross, which freed us from the Evil One.[5]

1. Gn 1:2
2. Ezk 36:25
3. Ezk 47:1-2; Rv 22:1-2
4. Jn 3:5
5. 1 Cor 12:13; Rv 22:1

Water which cleanses and wells up in eternal life.

HOLY OILS

WHEN AN ANOINTED OIL PENETRATES THE FLESH,
THE SPIRIT OF GOD DESCENDS INTO THE MIDST OF OUR HEARTS

IN EVERY AGE, MANKIND, AND MEN OFTEN JUST AS MUCH AS WOMEN, HAVE ADORED PERFUMES AND UNGUENTS. THE SCRIPTURES talk about oil as a true symbol of joy, which sets faces shining.[1]

As it penetrates and fills the flesh, an anointment with oil symbolizes the consecration of a person by God into the role of being a king, priest or prophet. Objects and buildings can also be consecrated by anointment. Our greatest example of the Anointed is the Messiah or Christ, two words which in Hebrew and Greek are used for Jesus, the King, High Priest and Prophet. His strength and beauty is celebrated thus in one of the psalms: "You love uprightness and detest evil. This is why God, your God, has anointed you with oil of gladness, as none of your rivals" (Ps 45:7).

Oil is a symbol of joy and beauty, and hence of consecration, but it is also a balm (or an ointment as we would now say) which relieves pain and strengthens wrestlers, making them suppler and less vulnerable. From this varied symbolism, the Church has concentrated on three types of oil, known as the "holy oils": the *oil of the catechumens* gives the strength of the Holy Spirit to those who are going to be baptized and become the wrestlers of God, beside Christ, against the spirit of Evil; the *oil of anointing* is the

outward sign (the substance) used in the sacrament of the anointing of the sick as unction for the forehead and the palms of the hands—it relieves the sick with the presence of the Holy Spirit; the *holy chrism* is a fragrant oil used for anointment during consecrations. After baptism, it marks the top of the head of the new son of God. During confirmation, it crosses the forehead. After an episcopal ordination, it is rubbed into the top of the new bishop's head; similarly, the hands of a new priest are anointed with it. During the dedication of churches and altars, it is spread over the crosses of consecration and all across the table of the altar. On each of these occasions, anointment with the holy chrism symbolizes the intervention of the Holy Spirit, which takes possession of beings or objects according to their mission or function.

It is during the "chrism" mass on the morning of Maundy Thursday that the bishop solemnly blesses the oil of the catechumens and the oil of anointing before finally consecrating the holy chrism. The priests who celebrate this mass with him extend their hands during the consecration of the holy chrism. The holy oils are then kept in silver or golden ampullae, or altar-cruets, which are often topped by a small cross.

1. Ps 104:15

The ampullae or altar-cruets containing the holy oils.

THE ROSARY

IN THE CONSTANT REPETITION OF THE "HAIL MARY"
WE ENTER INTO THE MYSTERIES OF JESUS THROUGH THE
MATERNAL TENDERNESS OF THE VIRGIN

DEVOTION TO THE VIRGIN MARY, THE MOTHER OF GOD, IS A CHARACTERISTIC OF THE CATHOLIC AND ALSO OF THE ORTHODOX Churches. Protestants consider that giving to the Mother is to take away from the Son, and that turning to Mary is an offence to Christ's universal power as mediator, even though Our Lady is entirely dependent on Our Lord.

The most widespread form of Marian devotion is without doubt the rosary, which can be found in any Catholic's hands until the day he dies. This "rose-garden" (from the Latin *rosarium*) is a crown intended to honour the Virgin Mother. It consists of five sets of ten beads, separated by an individual bead, which are an invitation to fifty recitations of "Hail Mary", five of "Our Father", and five of "Glory be to the Father." The rosary also has a sort of tail, finishing with a cross, which carries three successive beads with two individual beads, one at each end. On the cross, which is in fact the starting point, we recite the "I believe in God"; on the first individual bead the "Our Father", then three "Hail Marys" and finally a "Glory be to the Father." The rosary thus honours the Trinity, the Cross and the Virgin at the same time, all fundamental Catholic truths.

This lesser rosary is only a part of the full rosary. To tell the Rosary is to offer Our Lady a garland of roses made up of three lesser rosaries. The Feast of the Holy Rosary, on October 7, is related to the naval victory of the Christians over the Turkish fleet at Lepanto in October, 1571.

The "Hail Mary"—or the *Ave Maria*—is also known as the "angelic salutation" because it recalls the salutation of the Angel Gabriel to Mary at the Annunciation, to which can be added Elizabeth's salutation during the Visitation.[1] The second part of the prayer is not taken directly from the Gospels: "Holy Mary, Mother of God, pray for us sinners now and at the hour of our death. Amen." When recited in privacy or communally certain variants exist, in particular the addition of "petitions", which dwell on the mysteries which are meditated in the first part.

It is a matter of entering into the mysteries of salvation through the proximity of Mary's heart.[2] The three crowns of the rosary are consecrated to the joyous mysteries, the sorrowful mysteries and the glorious mysteries. Like the 150 psalms, these 150 *Ave Maria* are a study in contemplation. They allow us to enter, through the heart of a Mother entirely given over to the Spirit of Love, into the designs which, through her Son, the Father has conceived for us.

1. Lk 1:28,42
2. Lk 2:19,51

A rosary hanging from the belt of a Dominican's robe.

THE LITURGICAL CALENDAR

WITHIN THE TEMPORAL CYCLE OF DAYS, WEEKS AND YEARS,
THE SUCCESSION OF FESTIVALS AND SAINTS' DAYS
BRING US EVER CLOSER TO GOD

EVEN IF THE ANCIENTS DID NOT CORRECTLY UNDERSTAND THE MOVEMENTS OF THE STARS AND PLANETS, AND BELIEVED THAT THE Earth was the centre of the universe, they were perfectly familiar with the rotation of the seasons, dividing the year into twelve months and observing the close proximity of certain planets, which they linked with their mythological gods.

When the Roman Empire abandoned its old system of dating by means of the Kalends, Nones and Ides, replacing it with a seven day week which they took from the Egyptians, these gods were used to name their days: Sunday was the Day of the Sun (*solis dies*, in German *Sonntag*); Monday was the day of the Moon (in French *lundi*); Tuesday was the day of Mars (in French *mardi*), who in English has been replaced by his Norse equivalent Tiw, the god of war; Wednesday was the day of Mercury (in French *mercredi*), in English replaced by his equivalent Woden; Thursday was the day of Jupiter (in French *jeudi*) replaced by Thor, the god of thunder; Friday was the day of Venus (in French *vendredi*), who was replaced by the goddess Frig; and Saturday was Saturn's day. Hours were counted according to the solar day which breaks down into four groups of three hours.

The Bible has put its own understanding of the cosmos in the place of these polytheistic religions. According to Genesis, the sun and the moon are nothing more than instruments intended to divide light from darkness; the stars and the planets are the armies of the Lord of Sabaoth, they cannot be worshipped in any way. The first six days of the week correspond to the successive stages of the creation, and the seventh is that of divine rest. That is why, for the Jews, Saturn's day is the Sabbath (from the Hebrew *shabbath*, "rest"; a Greek variant of this word turned it into *sambati dies*, hence the French *samedi* and the German *Samstag*).

The Christians called the first day of the week, Sunday, the "Day of the Lord" (*dies dominicus*, hence the French *dimanche*) in honour of the Resurrection. It also perpetuates certain ancient symbols, for the shining of the sun, which is born again each morning, is associated with the image of the Risen Christ; this metaphor was derived from the Old Testament.[1] The Virgin Mary who is not, like her Son, "light from light" (*Credo*) but reflects his brightness, obviously finds her role of mediator symbolized by the moon; numerous painters at all periods have represented her with her feet resting on a crescent moon.

Paschal Candle in a twelfth-century candlestick in Saint Clement's, Rome.

From a delicate interweaving of this succession of different beliefs and symbols, as well as the different way in which time was measured, the three cycles of Catholic liturgy finally emerged: the daily cycle, the weekly cycle, and the yearly cycle. The daily liturgical cycle of "Hours" is made up of prayers, psalms and readings which sanctify the various moments of the day: Lauds in the morning, the noontide office, Vespers at the end of the afternoon, and Compline before going to bed. The "Books of Hours", of which superb examples come down from the Middle Ages, are collections of prayers which allow laymen to follow these rituals. There are also nocturnal vigils (or Matins) for monks and nuns, and the "Little Hours", inspired by the Jewish tradition, which still follow the divisions of the day that were used in antiquity: tierce (about 10 a.m.), sext (about 1 p.m.) and nones (about 3 p.m.).

The weekly cycle starts on Sunday,[2] which is at once its source and its peak, hence the importance of Sunday mass for Catholics. From Monday to Saturday, each day follows its own liturgy from the second to the seventh *feria* (in Latin, "feast", for each and every day is sacred; this liturgical nomenclature goes back to the Later Byzantine Empire during which a vain attempt was made to ban the old pagan names for the days of the week). Friday, the day on which Our Lord died, is a day of penance and abstinence, which has made it unlucky in popular superstition.

The yearly cycle is more complicated, because it is simultaneously made up of the celebration of various liturgical moments in time (the "temporal") and the festivals of saints, which have been increasingly multiplied by popular devotion. But the mysteries of the Incarnation and Redemption are celebrated in the temporal cycle, which is thus of more importance. The Second Vatican Council made sure of re-establishing its primacy.

The temporal consists of two important cycles, Christmas and Easter, the celebration of which allows us to explore the entire mystery of our salvation in Christ. They both start with a time of preparation, Advent and Lent respectively, are centred on the Feast of the Nativity and the Paschal Triduum, continue with "Christmastide" and "Eastertide", before finishing with the Feast of the Baptism of Our Lord and with Pentecost. The rest of the year consists of thirty-four weeks of "Ordinary Time".

Here then, in chronological order, are the main festivals of the temporal cycles, with explanations of their meanings:

I. ADVENT - (from the Latin *adventus*, "coming"): the liturgical cycle begins with a time of preparation for Christmas, starting on the fourth Sunday before December 25. Advent is, for us, a time of joyous waiting (particularly on the third Sunday, which is called *Gaudete*, "rejoice", from the first word of its introit) for a triple coming: the humble birth of Jesus in a stable in Bethlehem, the grace which is still today given to us by celebrating his liturgy, and Christ's return in

Contemporary Christmas crib figures made by the Sisters of Bethlehem. Following double page: a mosaic of the Epiphany (thirteenth century) in the church of Santa Maria on the Transteverine, Rome.

glory on the last day. The first Sundays of Advent are focused on the third event, while the week immediately before Christmas concentrates on the other two.

II. CHRISTMAS -(or Noël, from the Latin *natalis dies*, "the day of birth"): nine months after the Annunciation (March 25), December 25 celebrates the birth of Christ and the mystery of the Incarnation, the basis of all Christian symbolism. Christmas is also the festival of the Holy Family of Joseph, Mary and Jesus, and so of all families, a celebration of life which comes from God before returning to him.

The solemnity of Christmas christianized the pagan festival of *Natalis Invicti* ("birth of the unconquered Sun") at the winter solstice. On that date, the sun starts to climb back up the sky, like the Child who is destined to grow up. Reciprocally, the summer solstice, on June 24, corresponds to the festival of Saint John the Baptist, the Precursor, who said of Jesus: "He must grow greater, I must grow less" (Jn 3:30).

III. EPIPHANY - (from the Greek *epi-phainein*, "to show, or reveal"): in the East, the feast of the Epiphany was the celebration of Jesus's birth and revelation as the Messiah and Saviour. Fixed on January 6, it is the festival of the True Light, that of the star which appeared to the Wise Men and guided them to Christ.[3] The feast of the Kings remains popular. In every crib, three "Magi" come to adore the true King and give him gold, frankincense and myrrh. Twelfth-night cake, which is blessed at the mass, symbolizes Christ, bread and life (in Hebrew, "Bethlehem" means "the house

of bread"). The Wise Men have rather eclipsed the two other "revelations" which Epiphany also celebrates: the baptism of Christ in the Jordan by John the Baptist (a feast day is consecrated to this on the Sunday after Epiphany, which concludes the Christmas cycle), and the Wedding at Cana, where his first public action took place.

IV. CANDLEMAS: on February 2, forty days after his birth, the Lord's Presentation at the Temple of Jerusalem is a complement to the Christmas cycle. This was an old Jewish custom, which the Holy Family respected.[4] It is a celebration of light, in connection with the words of old Simeon, who saw in the child "a light of revelation for the gentiles". It consists in a blessing and procession of candles before mass. The faithful, who hope to become "children of light" generally carry holy candles with them. These are then burnt beside the dead, as a sign of hope for eternal life.

V. LENT - (from the Old English *lencten*, "the spring"): this "holy quarantine" of forty days is a time of penitential preparation for Easter. The period of forty days is the same as that which preceded the meeting with God on Mount Sinai for both Moses and Elijah.[5] Jesus himself prepared for his public ministry by fasting in the desert for forty days.[6] Lent lasts for six weeks but, since penance is not performed on Sundays, it begins on the Wednesday before the first Sunday, that is on Ash Wednesday.

Its "ashes", normally obtained from burning the previous year's palms from Palm Sunday, symbolize mankind's worthlessness when faced with God. Following original sin, dust is the image of

A bouquet of box leaves for Palm Sunday.

118

death, linked with sin: "For dust you are" God said to the first man, "and to dust you shall return" (Gn 3:19). The practice of fasting also allows us to explore the limits of our human condition. As an antidote to overeating, it asks us to discover ourselves as beings dependent on our Creator's goodness.

In the middle of Lent, the fourth Sunday, which is called *Laetare* ("rejoice", the first word of the introit), marks a pause. The Church invites us to a joyful break before Easter. The great festival's white vestments are still to be donned, but the violet of penance brightens into pink.

The sixth Sunday of Lent is Palm Sunday, which starts Holy Week. It commemorates the solemn entry of Jesus into Jerusalem, a few days before his Passion and death on the Cross.[7] The congregation meets somewhere outside the church. Here, the celebrant blesses the palms (or branches of boxwood or bay, according to different regions) and a procession sets off towards the church for a mass, during which one of the Gospel accounts of the Passion is read. The faithful take home these branches which have been blessed and use them to decorate their crucifixes.

VI. EASTER - (from *Eastre*, a goddess whose festival was held at the spring equinox; the adjective "paschal" comes from the Hebrew *pasach*, "to spare", hence *pesach* "paschal-lamb", in Latin *pascha*; the sacrifice of the paschal-lamb being the prelude to the escape from Egypt): the Easter festival is the most important of the entire liturgical year and includes the three days of the paschal *Triduum*. It begins with a mass on the evening of Maundy Thursday, which commemorates the Last Supper, during which Jesus instituted the Eucharist. On the next day, Good Friday, we celebrate his Passion and death on the Cross, particularly during the afternoon office.

Apart from the liturgy itself, we also perform the ritual of the way of the Cross, with its fourteen stations which go from Jesus's condemnation to his burial; it can also be followed from the Last Supper until the Resurrection. Easter Saturday is a day of silence, of waiting and of hope. The celebration of the Resurrection begins with the Easter Vigil on Saturday evening, with the blessing of the newly kindled fire and of the Paschal Candle, followed by some lengthy readings and a mass. It inaugurates the Solemnity of Solemnities which constitutes the Easter festival, bearing witness to Jesus's victory over death in token of our own resurrection.

Easter is a movable feast, the date of which is not fixed by the civil calendar. According to the rules which were established in the fourth century, it is celebrated on the first Sunday after the fourteenth day following the new moon in March; that is to say, between March 22 at the earliest and April 25 at the latest. Each year, the entirety of the Easter cycle is fixed according to the date of Easter Day, which is introduced into the succession of the thirty-four ordinary Sundays.

The fifty days of the Easter period, which continue up to Pentecost, do not in reality contain more than one day of celebration, which is a time of joy and gladness, dominated by the chanting of Alleluia (from the Hebrew *halleluyah*, "praise Jah", that is to say "praise be to

The dove of the Holy Spirit in the centre of the Glory of Bernini (apse in Saint Peter's, Rome).

Yahweh, praise the Lord"), an acclamation which can be found in the Psalms.

VII. THE ASCENSION: forty days after Easter, the Ascension celebrates the final going up to heaven of the risen Lord. According to the Acts of the Apostles, Jesus, now victorious over death, appeared to his disciples for forty days during which he would "tell them about the kingdom of God" (Acts 1:3). As it is expressed in the creed: "He ascended into heaven and is seated at the right hand of the Father. He will come again in glory to judge the living and the dead, and his Kingdom will have no end."

VIII. PENTECOST - (from the Greek *pentekoste*, "the fiftieth [day]"): the fiftieth day after Easter, Pentecost is the festival which concludes Eastertide and, with the gift of the Spirit, it is the culmination of its mystery. The apostles were together with Mary in the Upper Room when they were filled with the Spirit, which came down on them as a violent wind and as tongues of fire which came to rest on their heads.[8] The fire of divine love could henceforth be spread by them, according to the mission which Jesus had given them. Pentecost is the day of the inception of the Church, which was born in their preaching concerning the marvels of God (Acts 2:11).

IX. TRINITY: the Sunday after Pentecost is the Festival of the Trinity, which comes late in the liturgy because the mystery of the unity of the Father, the Son and the Holy Spirit is the begin-

ning and end of the entire Christian life. It is constantly being celebrated (cf. the chapter dealing with the Trinity).

X. CORPUS CHRISTI DAY: on the Thursday after the Festival of the Trinity (or on the Sunday in certain countries and regions), Corpus Christi Day celebrates the Eucharist. It is a popular festival, marked by the worshipping and procession of the Holy Sacrament. The route which the Lord is to take is strewn with foliage and also decorated with designs made from dyed sawdust. Several towns throughout the world are famous for their magnificent processions.

XI. THE SACRED HEART: this festival is celebrated on the second Friday after Trinity Sunday. It is based around the idea of Christ's human love, and was suggested by the episode during which his heart was pierced after his death on the Cross.[9] The water and blood which flowed from that wound symbolize the sacraments, which spring everlastingly from Jesus's open heart.

XII. THE ASSUMPTION: the Virgin Mary's ascent into heaven, where she rejoins her Son in both body and spirit, is celebrated on August 15. As opposed to Christ, who ascended into the sky on his own, the Virgin was borne up by angels in the glory of God. This explains the word "Assump-tion" (from the Latin *assumere*, "to lift up, to raise").

XIII. ALL SAINTS' DAY: since the ninth century, November 1 has been a celebration of the

A nineteenth-century monstrance from the treasures of the abbey church of Paimpont (Ile-et-Vilaine, France). The Lamb and the seven seals can be seen on the base.

memory of all the saints, and it is a joyous anticipation of our own salvation. The next day, November 2, is consecrated to All Souls, which is sometimes mistakenly confused with All Saints' Day. This commemoration of the dead was founded by Saint Odilon, Abbot of Cluny, at the beginning of the sixth century.

XIV. CHRIST THE KING: since 1925 we have, on the thirty-fourth and last Sunday of Ordinary Time, celebrated The Feast of Christ the King, a solemn homage to him who gave himself completely for us, even to death. It is a preparation for the new liturgical year, which begins with Advent on the following Sunday.

Throughout the year, we also celebrate saints' days, whose memorials, feasts and solemnities are part of a different cycle. Each day is thus the occasion to remember different saints from various periods, whose merits can be a guide to Christians on the path towards perfection. Some of these days are more important than others, depending on the country or church; particularly the celebrations of "patron saints" of different churches or regions. There are also many firmly established popular traditions such as, in France, *les feux de Saint Jean* on Midsummer's Day, or the various sayings which have become attached to saints' days.

These different cycles which interweave and follow one another should not create the impression that Christians go round in circles. On the contrary, each year, each week and each day, they enter more fully into the essential mysteries of religion. Our nature as human beings means that we need these sorts of reminders, which let the grace and great love of God dwell more deeply in our hearts.

Liturgical cycles are signalled by the ringing of bells, which hence have an important place in the life of Christians. When they sound a baptism, marriage or funeral, the daily or Sunday masses and, in monasteries, the hours of the divine offices, the pealing of bells from a church is a sign of its vitality. Bells symbolize God calling to his people to celebrate the Covenant and also, traditionally, the voices of angels; this explains the veneration they have always received and the solemnity that surrounds their blessing which is, in a way, their baptism with an ablution, anointment with holy chrism and burning of incense.

1. "But for you who fear my name, the Sun of justice will rise with healing in his rays." (Mal 3:20)
2. "On the first day of the week, at the first sign of dawn, they went to the tomb." (Lk 24:1)
3. Mt 2:1-12
4. Lv 12:2-4; Lk 2:22-38
5. Ex 24:18; 1 Kgs 19:8
6. Mt 4:2
7. "The great crowd of people who had come up for the festival heard that Jesus was on his way to Jerusalem. They took branches of palm and went out to receive him . . . " (Jn 12:12-13)
8. Acts 2:1-13
9. Jn 19:32-34

An embroidered Sacred Heart. Following page: Saint Peter, Saint Cornelius and Saint Calepode. Twelfth-century mosaic in the church of Santa Maria on the Transteverine, Rome.

CONCLUSION

THE SYMBOL OF THE FAITH

The pages which you have just read and looked at present an explanation of the most important symbols of the Catholic Church. What we have endeavoured to do through this illustrated book is provide an introduction to Christian symbolism for all those who seek a deeper knowledge of their own religion, or that of other believers. As with the other books in this collection, it attempts to be both open and respectful, and so is part of the call which John Paul II has made to the various religions' faithful.

As you will already have seen, the symbols of Catholicism, despite their diversity, revolve essentially around the redeeming Incarnation of Jesus Christ, who is God made man and who came to unite God's scattered children. At an early age, the word "symbol" in the Christian tradition came to mean a condensed profession of faith by which the faithful could recognize one another. The *Credo* was to become their deepest sign of communication; it was no longer a question of bringing together two pieces of a single object (the Greek *symbolon*) in order to express the relationship between the two people that possessed them, but rather to affirm the essential parts of their shared faith. Two symbols thus express the Church's faith: the Apostles' Creed, which goes back to the earliest signs of a belief in the Trinity tied in with baptism, and what is known as the Nicæo-Constantinopolitan Creed (from the two Councils which were held respectively in 325 and 381), both of which are part of the Sunday mass.

The various symbols—or symbolized truths—which have been presented here come together in the Symbol of Faith, or Creed. Its structure is trinitarian: it proceeds from the almighty Father, the creator of the visible world and the invisible (represented by the angels); it progresses in the redemptive Incarnation which comes from Mary's consent and which culminates in the Passion, death, resurrection and ascension of Jesus; the fruit of these divine works is the gift of the Holy Spirit which creates a Church provided with sacraments to transmit that Creed.

As such, in its various articles (and in the way they are expressed) it above all attests to the organic unity of all Christian symbols; how, in their daily use, from the sign of the cross to the application of holy water or incense, they express and nurture the communion of the Church, of the "People unified by the Trinity."

ACKNOWLEDGMENTS

I should first like to thank **Cardinal Jean-Marie Lustiger**, Archbishop of Paris, for the confidence he showed in asking me to write this book. I am thankful to my community for its support and for the way it took this mission to heart. I accepted the task with the conviction that it could serve as a modern evangelistic tool, helping the younger generations to discover, or rediscover, their spiritual roots.

The initial idea came from **Editions Assouline**, known for their high-quality art books: a thank-you to the entire team for their inspirational efficiency. Working with a photographer was a new experience for me and has been extremely enriching, particularly in the company of **Laziz Hamani**, whose use of light makes us see things with new eyes; his assistant, Philippe Sebirot, was constantly a friendly and efficient helpmate. In Brittany, Paris and Rome, the three of us formed a happy triumvirate.

Monsieur l'Abbé Robert Daniel, Rector of Carnac (Morbihan), welcomed us to his beautiful church of Saint-Cornély, where we photographed the font. Monsieur l'Abbé Alain Rebour, Priest-in-Charge of the abbey church of Paimpont (Ile-et-Vilaine), in the very heart of the Forest of Brocéliande, gave us access to the collection of relics, and allowed us to photograph an extremely fine crucifix dating from the seventeenth or eighteenth centuries and a beautifully crafted monstrance from the nineteenth; we also shot the Trinity on the altarpiece, which dates from the seventeenth century.

In Paris, **Monsieur l'Abbé Patrick Chauvet**, Rector of the basilica of the Sacré-Cœur in Montmartre, gave a warm welcome to our photographers, and several images here published bear witness to that. **Mother Marie-France**, Superior of the Missionary Sisters of Charity, allowed us, with the permission of **Mother Theresa**, to photograph a young Indian sister.

In Rome, **Cardinal Paul Poupard**, President of the Pontifical Council for Culture, who presided at the ordination of priests in Kergonan on August 5, 1995, which is depicted here, was kind enough to receive us and show us round the Eternal City. **Doctor Marjorie Weeke**, delegate of the Pontifical Council for Social Communication, procured the necessary passes for us to be able to take photographs during the closing mass of the Special Assembly of the Synod of Bishops for Lebanon, presided over by **Pope John Paul II** in the basilica of Saint Peter's on December 14, 1995, as well as at other masses in the Vatican during the following days.

Monsignor David Lewis, Vicar Capitular of the basilica of Santa Maria Maggiore, was kind enough to allow photographs to be taken during the Sunday mass of *Gaudete*, conducted by **Cardinal Ugo Poletti**. **Reverend Father Leonard Boyle**, o.p., welcomed us warmly when we photographed the beautiful mosaics and ambo of the *schola*.

Back in Brittany, **Monsieur l'Abbé Jean Le Dorze**, Rector of the basilica of Sainte-Anne d'Auray, where the Pope came in pilgrimage in September of this year, 1996, kindly gave us access to his chapel for the posed photographs of liturgical gestures.

Finally, I should like to give my warm thanks to the scholar **Bernard Huchet** for his friendly assistance during the revision of this text, which is destined for a wider public.

My thanks, too, to **Alitalia** for its contributions; to **Corinne de Craecker**, who gave her friendly help at every stage of this book; and to **Marie Viloin, Daniel Delisle** of the Prunelle Studio, the shops **Cheret, art sacré** and **Art et Religion** in Paris, for their help in producing this book.